BILL
GATES

BILL GATES

CHRIS MCNAB

PICTURE CREDITS

Alamy: 19, 44, 49, 75, 105, 118, 120, 123, 128, 131, 135, 142, 145, 148

Public domain: 28

Shutterstock: 151, 153, 187

This edition published in 2024 by Arcturus Publishing Limited
26/27 Bickels Yard, 151–153 Bermondsey Street,
London SE1 3HA

AD010860UK

Printed in the UK

MIX
Paper | Supporting
responsible forestry
FSC® C171272

CONTENTS

Introduction 7

Chapter 1 Finding The Drive 15
Chapter 2 The Microsoft Phenomenon 41
Chapter 3 From Word To Windows 71
Chapter 4 New Times, Harder Times 101
Chapter 5 Giving Back 137
Chapter 6 Who Is Bill Gates? 169

Bibliography 196
Index 206

INTRODUCTION

History books are replete with individuals who have exerted an above-average influence on human affairs. The fields in which they do so are many and varied – politics, military leadership, religion, medicine, technology, exploration, literature, art, philosophy, architecture, and many others. Defining what unites them all, beyond simply being high achievers, isn't altogether straightforward. Put simply, they aren't all the same.

Biographies of entrepreneurial lives reveal wide variations in personal circumstances and psychological make-up. The wealth and stability of their upbringing (or lack of it); parental relationships; educational performance; romantic involvements; chosen career or business type. These and multiple other factors vary between the business big-hitters. But one outstanding factor seems to unite them all. In their respective fields of endeavour, they demonstrate a drive to succeed, expressed in a crushing work ethic, which usually goes beyond what is typical in the general run of humanity. They do whatever it takes. The pathological pursuit of success is not always pretty – the stand-out figures of history have ranged from the sublimely moral to egregiously amoral, with every shade and hue in between. Achievement and harmony are, as we shall see, not always happy bedfellows.

This book is about one figure of recent history who belongs at or near the summit in the pantheon of high achievers – Bill

Gates. To rescue that statement from sycophancy, I base it not on his personal qualities (although they will certainly be part of the equation), but on rather cold mathematics of influence. On a utilitarian scale, measured purely by the number of individuals affected, Bill Gates has had a greater *practical* impact on everyday humanity than most other leading figures of history. Almost every person on the planet beyond infancy knows who Bill Gates is. And almost every person who has used or benefited from computers since the early 1980s will have come into contact with one of his products. Given what computers have done to shape the very nature of the modern world, Gates' global effect, therefore, is truly profound.

We need a little more justification here. Bill Gates as an individual did not, by any means, invent personal computing. He didn't invent hardware or software, operating systems, programming languages, graphical user interfaces, memory disks, hard drives, nor countless other elements of computing paraphernalia. What he did, however, was drive computing into the hands of the masses with almost inconceivable success and scale.

Gates was the co-founder (with Paul Allen) of the world's most successful technology company, Microsoft. Microsoft's climb to greatness is both a personal history centred on Bill Gates and a wider corporate narrative. But viewed from any angle, it is an astonishing story. This initially tiny, scrappy enterprise grew from having little but raw ambition to being one of the most unimaginably wealthy and socially impactful companies in history, with annual revenues peaking at more than $200 billion and a corporate worth that topped $2 trillion in June 2021 (that value is still climbing). Against numerous strong rivals in the emerging computing market of the 1970s and 1980s (including future behemoths such as Apple), Microsoft aggressively clawed market share in programming language development, then in operating systems, then in software applications.

But it was the launch of MS Windows in 1985 that fired the starting gun on Microsoft's race towards dominance of the global personal computing market. After an initial sticky start, as Gates and Microsoft attempted to perfect the product and iron out its many bugs, Windows gained traction over the course of its updates, then went stratospheric in terms of its adoption and commercial success. At the peak of that imperium in 2013, MS Windows had 90.96 per cent market share in computer desktop operating systems (DOS). Layered on top of that were Microsoft's world-beating applications, most running on both Windows and Apple computers. They included Word, Excel and PowerPoint, collectively bundled together with other productivity software in MS Office. Ask any computer-using human being on the planet in the 1990s or first decades of the 2000s to close their eyes and think about a computer interface, and it is almost guaranteed that they would picture the colours, menus, sounds, icons and settings of Microsoft products. By playing the leading role in the global distribution of affordable software, Microsoft essentially democratized computing and fuelled the digital revolution.

To this picture we can add some further overlays of Microsoft products and influence. It became a central player in the gaming market through its Xbox games console, introduced in November 2001. For a time, it was a contender in the cell phone market, although, as we shall discover, its forays into both phone hardware and mobile operating systems constitutes one of Microsoft's biggest failures. By contrast, Microsoft's cloud computing platform, Azure, is today one of the world's biggest digital service platforms. Microsoft is also now one of the key figures behind the wildly accelerating development of Artificial Intelligence (AI) systems, most prominently in the form of the ChatGPT interface, which is being merged into Microsoft's Bing search engine.

Let's pause for a moment and think about what this all means. By 2015, there were more than 2 billion computers in the world. The vast majority of them were running Microsoft Windows and using its software. Now summon to mind just some of the possible activities enabled by that software – data analysis, bookkeeping, financial planning, process design, letter writing, emailing, maintaining records, writing novels, organizing information, searching the internet, administrating public services. There are countless others. But putting these elements together, we can confidently say that the modern digital world has largely been built upon Microsoft. There are few individuals on the planet whose lives have not been touched, at least indirectly, by the use of Microsoft products. This remains true today in 2024, even with Windows' market share falling to about 73 per cent.

The story of Microsoft is inseparable from that of Bill Gates, whose personal and corporate journey we will explore in this book. There is some controversy embedded in this story, especially regarding the degree to which he shaped the software and applications that bore the Microsoft name. As an experiment to prove this point, try typing the admittedly loaded search string 'Bill Gates didn't invent anything' into a search engine. Not only will this phrase almost certainly auto-complete before you get to the end of typing it, but it will throw up many, many results declaiming Gates and relegating his career to riding on the backs of inventive others.

If we look at Microsoft purely in terms of its software coding, there is a degree of truth in this proposition. Bill Gates did not single-handedly invent Microsoft's products, including foundational elements of Microsoft's technical evolution, such as the BASIC programming language (invented by John G. Kemeny and Thomas E. Kurtz at Dartmouth College in 1963), graphical user interface (GUI, courtesy of Xerox), MS-DOS (from Seattle Computer Products' 86-DOS, in turn derived from Digital Research's CP/M) and the computer mouse (Apple, among others). Even Windows, that archetype of Microsoft identity, resulted in a lawsuit brought by Apple against Microsoft over alleged copyright violations of Macintosh GUI elements. The idea that Gates did not have a creative role in Microsoft's evolution most sensationally crystallized in the voice of Gates' arch competitor, the late and equally great Steve Jobs, who in his defining biography by Walter Isaacson declared: 'Bill is basically unimaginative and has never invented anything, which is why I think he's more comfortable now in philanthropy than technology ... He just shamelessly ripped off other people's ideas.' (Isaacson 2011: 173).

Across its chapters, this book will form a strong argument against this position. (As will emerge, there was considerable ill-tempered historical baggage between Gates and Jobs by the time Jobs made this statement.) Without Bill Gates – without his intelligence, technical know-how, near-limitless energy, entrepreneurial drive, digital vision, ruthless competitive spirit, and many other factors – there would possibly be no Microsoft, or at least a much-reduced version of it. Critics can sometimes home in on the protean act of pure invention but ignore the grinding daily effort that is arguably more impressive – taking the boulder of invention and pushing it relentlessly uphill until it becomes a success, an act of Herculean will and adaptive intelligence against endless obstacles and gleeful opposition.

Gates could be seen as first among equals in this regard. He built Microsoft into the world's defining computer company with a focus, ambition and intelligence that remain legendary. He rose to become the world's wealthiest individual, a position that he held for many years. (In January 2024, at the time of writing, he was ranked the eighth wealthiest person, with Elon Musk, Bernard Arnault, Jeff Bezos in the top three.) Although he stepped down from day-to-day running of Microsoft in 2008, and gave up his board position in 2020, his name is still indelibly imprinted upon the Microsoft brand. Given the sheer influence of Microsoft products outlined earlier, it is almost hard to imagine what the modern world would look like were it not for Bill Gates.

Today, Gates' detractors have new horizons. Gates' wealth, influence, ideas and status have attracted the wildest species of conspiracy theories, not least the idea that Gates used the coronavirus vaccination programme to implant miniaturized 5G trackers inside millions of the world's citizens. (For what purpose in unclear, given that the cell phones most of the world willingly carries around are far more effective personalized trackers.) Disregarding such feverish concoctions, we must acknowledge that Bill Gates has now punched well beyond the Microsoft legacy to become a global philanthropic influence that eclipses most other billionaires. By the end of 2021, the Bill & Melinda Gates Foundation (BMGF), founded in 2000, had made $65.5 billion in development grant payments, the larger of the foundation endowments coming from direct transfers of personal wealth from Bill and Melinda. Working across 144 countries, and tackling continent-changing economic, health and social issues, it may well be in the distant future that Gates is as much associated with reformist achievements as with digital entrepreneurship. A complex, divisive and exceptional figure, Bill Gates has a relevance to the modern world that cannot be denied.

SOME KEY TERMS

Much of this book deals with the rise of Microsoft in the age of personal computing. As such, it is useful to have at least a basic grasp of some of the core technical concepts within that industry, not least because they will have a central relevance to understanding Bill Gates' relationship to the computer revolution. The following are some of these key concepts, but further guidance can be found through works in the Bibliography:

Central Processing Unit (CPU) Also central processor or microprocessor. The CPU is a physical component in a computer that takes instructions from a software program or an item of hardware and facilitates their execution.

Compiler A program that translates a programming language's source code into machine code, byte code or another programming language. Essentially, a compiler allows the computer to run a program without having the software needed to create the program.

Graphical User Interface An interactive interface in which the user triggers computer actions by interacting (usually via a mouse or keyboard) with icons and other visual symbols that represent programs, menus and other features.

Interpreter A program that reads, translates and executes an uncompiled computer program in real time.

Programming language A computer language that is used by developers to create instructions for computers to execute, often in the form of software programs or scripts.

Source code In computer programming, the code or language used to create the program.

Syntax Essentially the 'grammar' of the programming language, the set of rules about how it is written, structured and spelled.

CHAPTER 1
FINDING THE DRIVE

In the world of entrepreneurial biographies, there is a rags-to-riches sub-genre. The individuals on this library shelf are those who have clawed their way from the very bottom to the very top, driving themselves out of austerity and adversity, overcoming countless obstacles placed in their way by the privileged, but by sheer grit making it to the top of their game. Such stories are absolutely and deservedly inspiring. But to the public, they can cloud the fact that poverty and disadvantage *are* extremely effective at stacking the chances against success. In many ways, they demonstrate the logic fallacy of 'survival bias', in which they draw conclusions based on the few individuals who survived a process of selection, while ignoring the negative outcomes of the mass of people who fell by the wayside, even though the winners might actually simply represent statistical outliers.

Conversely, the study of successful individuals does appear to show that stability, nurture and affluence in childhood and youth all turbocharge the possibility of a person's future achievement. A headline in the *Washington Post* in 2018 put it succinctly when it summarized new research: 'It's better to be born rich than gifted.' (Van Dam 2018). But in the case of Bill Gates, we might repackage this headline as: 'It's *best of all* to be born rich *and* gifted.' For regardless of his propitious surroundings in childhood, from his earliest years, Bill Gates exhibited personal qualities and intellectual capabilities that undoubtedly stacked the cards in his favour.

BACKGROUND

Gates came from confident, prominent stock. His father was William Henry Gates III (1925–2020) – also known as Bill Gates Sr. – a high flyer in business and law. As a young man, he had served for three years in the US Army during the second half of the Second World War, leaving the service with the rank of 1st lieutenant in 1946 (the year after the end of hostilities) and heading to law school at the University of Washington. Gates Sr. left university in 1950 with a Doctor of Jurisprudence degree and began making a name for himself in the legal profession, co-founding the law firm Shidler McBroom & Gates in 1964. This company in turn became Shidler McBroom Gates & Lucas by 1990, before a 1997 merger transformed it into Preston Gates & Ellis LLP (PGE), by which time Bill Gates Sr.'s son Bill Jr. had already become the world's richest man. Bill Sr. also became the president of the Washington State Bar Association. Winding back the story, however, Bill Sr. cut his teeth in the practice of corporate law, especially as it related to technology, a branch of law that would one day be especially useful to his son as he bounded through the minefields of digital intellectual property, copyright and contract agreements.

It was while at the University of Washington that Bill Gates Sr. met one Mary Ann Maxwell (1929–94), an engaging, outgoing and determined student born in Seattle (Gates Sr. was born about 90 minutes away from Seattle in Bremerton, Washington). Romance blossomed between the two, and they married in 1951. Mary was the scion of a prominent US family. Her grandfather and father had both been highly successful in the banking industry, her father rising to the prestigious heights of vice president of the Pacific National Bank. But although Mary was raised in generational affluence, it was of a restrained type – the family members didn't sit complacently on either their wealth or their laurels. Indeed, the family had something of a disdain for egregious displays of status or self-indulgent spending, a trait that Mary and Bill Sr. would pass on to their son.

Mary was a mover and shaker in her own right. Across her adult life, she glided gracefully and purposefully through the highest strata of society, business and philanthropy, fuelled by an ambitious spirit of volunteerism and community service. She served on the boards of many prominent non-profit organizations, including the Children's Hospital Foundation, Seattle Symphony, Greater Seattle Chamber of Commerce and the United Way of King County; in the latter she was the first female president and in 1983 became the first woman to chair the national United Way's executive committee. (United Way is one of the world's biggest non-profit international fundraising alliances: https://www.unitedway.org/.) She became a regent (an educational leadership position) of the University of Washington in 1975, serving her alma mater for 18 years through astute management of legal, financial and governance issues. Mary also had a crisp business acumen, working on the boards of major corporations such as the First Interstate Bank of Washington, Unigard Security Insurance Group, Pacific Northwest Bell Telephone Company and KIRO Inc.

In short, the young Bill Gates Jr. had absolutely no shortage of inspirational, proximate models for success and a high work ethic. More than that, for Bill Gates, family has been one of the great stabilizing and influencing factors in his life. Both his mother and father assisted with the early development of Microsoft in practical ways, but it is also evident that some of their character traits rubbed off on their son. James Wallace and Jim Erickson, authors of the recommended *Hard Drive: Bill Gates and the Making of the Microsoft Empire*, quoted a Seattle attorney who worked with Gates Sr. and defined him as 'a hard man, difficult and demanding' (Wallace and Erickson 1992: 15). Some of that steely character doubtless bore down upon Bill Jr. at times, but following his father's death in 2020 a post by Gates on LinkedIn reflected powerfully on both his father's character and Gates' relation to him:

> My father's death is a tremendous loss for our family and the many people whose lives he touched. Dad lived a long and enormously meaningful life. I never stopped learning from his wisdom, kindness, and humility. Melinda and I owe him a special debt because his commitment to serving the community and the world helped inspire our own philanthropy. Although he would be the last person to say it, my father's compassion and generosity will live on in the foundation he helped build. As I've said many times before, my dad was the real Bill Gates. He was all the things I strive to be.
> (Gates 2020)

The last sentence clearly sets out the extent to which Gates has attempted to model himself on his father. A longer, beautifully tender, reflection on his father's death in the 'GateNotes' blog (https://www.gatesnotes.com) spoke of the way that Gates and his sisters had the benefit of parents who gave 'constant encouragement' and unconditional love. Tragically, Gates' mother died in 1994 from breast cancer at the age of 64. In a 2019 Twitter post, Gates remembered her as 'one of the most generous people I've ever known'. In the swirling world of characters that have surrounded Gates throughout his life, it is clear that his parents acted as a stable, dependable anchor at the centre.

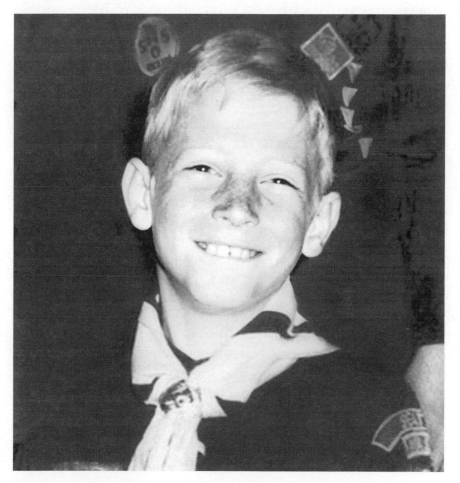

The young Bill Gates (here aged ten) was an active member of the Boy Scout movement.

Bill Gates Jr. – full name William Henry Gates III – was born in Seattle on 28 October 1955. He was the middle child of the family, bracketed by two sisters: an older sister Kristi (Kristianne) and a younger sister, Libby. Making a play on the 'III' after his name, and doubtless finding a way to avoid name confusion with his father, Bill acquired the nickname 'Trey'. He was also something of a happy infant, earning him the other nickname, 'Happy boy'.

Searching Gates' early years for signatures of future success requires caution, as everyday experience is replete with examples of failed promise. The young Gates was certainly very bright and deeply curious, an inquisitive nature strapped to a surplus of energy – he developed a signature physical mannerism of rocking his upper body when excited or agitated, a trait that survived into adulthood and to which those who worked closely with him became sensitive. In a three-part 2018 documentary for Netflix, Gates explained that despite his future closeness with his parents, there was a period of adolescence in which the relationship between the three of them was troubled. Gates became difficult, defiant and withdrawn, either ignoring his parents in his room or wilfully, cruelly, defying their authority. On one occasion, such was his rudeness to his mother at the dinner table that his father threw a full glass of water over him. The situation reached such a frustrating impasse that his parents arranged for Gates to see a counsellor. This process had a long-term benefit, as much as Gates resisted it initially. In the documentary, Gates spoke of how the counsellor wisely pointed out the inequality of the battle between him and his parents, specifically that he was prepared to inflict pain on them that they, as parents who loved him, would be unwilling to return. Gradually, Gates seems to have readjusted his focus and the closeness with his mother and father began to forge.

As Gates advanced through school, it became clear that he had exceptional intelligence and powers of memory, being able to absorb and retain knowledge of all types at a ferocious rate. Over time, this power became allied to a highly competitive nature. Whatever he did, Gates had to be the best, working out all the angles to do so. Here, Wallace and Erickson quote an old school friend of Gates: 'Bill loved playing pickleball and was fiercely competitive. He loved playing tennis and was fiercely competitive. He loved water skiing and was fiercely competitive. Everything he did, he did competitively and not simply to relax. He was a very driven individual.' (Wallace and Erickson 1992: 16).

By the end of Gates' junior school years, it was evident to his parents that their son required an environment that would stretch and challenge his mental development to the maximum. Thus in 1967, Bill Sr. and Mary enrolled Gates in Lakeside, the prestigious private all-boys prep school in Seattle, known for its reputation in imparting educational excellence and social polish. In a 1993 interview, Gates remembered that he initially applied a somewhat contorted efficiency–achievement model to his school life. During eighth grade he worked out a strategy for doing 'reasonably well without any effort' (Gates 1993). For any assignment, the school provided an 'effort' mark, scaled as 1, 2 or 3, and an accompanying grade mark. Gates notes that his ideal was 'A3', signifying the highest grade for the least amount of effort. This approach apparently gave mixed dividends, so Gates suddenly understood that more effort was required. From the ninth grade onwards he had 'a reasonably spotless grade record' (Ibid.).

At Lakeside, Gates would excel in almost every academic and most extra curricular domains. He showed talent and enthusiasm for maths and science, which provided the intellectual and logical cornerstones for much of what was to come. (He remains a passionate advocate for the study of both of these subjects.) But it was at Lakeside that Gates had a critical introduction to a technology that would, largely through his hands, come to change the nature of global society and business – Bill Gates met computers.

TECHNOLOGY FUTURES

It is worth diverting for a moment to orientate ourselves to the digital landscape of the late 1960s. Unlike tech entrepreneurs such as Elon Musk and Jeff Bezos, who rode the wave of the internet atop an already established personal computing industry, Gates grew up in a time in which computers were a rarity or an absence for the vast majority of the American population. This meant that his first experiences of computing were of hardware and software that stood on new-born, trembling legs, struggling to function and find purpose.

By 1967, when Gates entered Lakeside, computers were at the very beginning of the runway of commercial adoption. They were very large, very slow and very expensive, and thus were mostly the preserve of blue-chip corporations or major government/military institutions. Electronic digital programmable computers had first, famously, emerged with the wartime 'Colossus' computer, developed in the UK to accelerate decoding enciphered messages produced by the German Enigma cipher device. It was followed closely in the United States by the Electronic Numerical Integrator and Computer (ENIAC), which, with the ability to make 5,000 mathematical calculations every second, was primarily used to calculate artillery firing solutions for the US Army's Ballistic Research Laboratory.

These machines and their ilk were all very impressive for the immediate post-war years, but they had profound limitations. They were physically massive constructions, weighing many tons and filling the volume of a small room, great works of vacuum tubes, crystal diodes, relays, resistors and capacitors. Their programmable capability was not delivered through stored memory, but rather through days of time-consuming labour physically reconfiguring the system's thousands of wires and switches.

The next stage in the digital evolution was stored-program computers – computers that had the operating instructions actually built into the computer's memory rather than a vast spectrum of physical components. The advantages of such a device were manifold. They could perform multiple different functions without the machine needing to be rewired between each task, hence they were both more efficient and more flexible. Crucially for the future of Bill Gates, stored-program computers also offered the possibility of democratizing computer programming, opening it up to anyone who could acquire the relevant programming language.

The first examples of stored-program computers began to emerge in the late 1940s through ground-breaking devices with catchy names such as Manchester Baby, Manchester Mark 1, EDSAC and EDVAC. The first commercially available stored-program computer, the Ferranti Mark 1, emerged on to the market in February 1951. The 1950s also saw the rise of the International Business Machines (IBM) corporation. Its first purchasable computer, the IBM 701

Electronic Data Processing Machine, was announced to the public on 21 May 1952, although it was primarily intended for military use. The future dynamic interaction between this most sober of companies and the maverick, chaotic Microsoft is one of the most fascinating aspects of Gates' early commercial development.

All this was just the beginning and the 1950s witnessed an increasing expansion of hardware and software solutions. In 1955–59, US computer scientist, mathematician and US Navy rear admiral Grace Hopper oversaw the development of the FLOW-MATIC data processing language, which became the bedrock of the popular Common Business-Oriented Language (COBOL). (Hopper was later dubbed the 'First Lady of Software' in a 2016 posthumous Presidential Medal of Freedom citation.) The FORmula TRANslation (FORTRAN) programming language was created by IBM in 1954. In 1958, American electrical engineer Jack Kilby of Texas Instruments demonstrated the first working 'integrated circuit' (IC), what we would later call a 'microchip', a single miniaturized component containing a set of electrical circuits. The IC was improved materially and functionally by Robert Noyce at Fairchild Semiconductor, and thereafter the exponentially increasing power and decreasing size of ICs would open up the digital future.

By 1967, computers were being built around the new IC technology. The first 'minicomputers' had arrived on the scene with machines such as Digital Equipment Corporation's PDP-1 (Programmed Data Processor-1), introduced in 1960, and several IBM machines in the following years. ('Minicomputers' are defined as computers that are smaller, cheaper and less powerful than a large mainframe, but more expensive and more powerful than a personal computer.) IBM also introduced a magnetic disk storage drive – or hard disk – in 1962 (alongside several other data-storage innovations in the industry), while the following year saw the invention of the computer mouse. On 1 May 1964, and crucially for the future of Microsoft, developers John George Kemeny and Thomas Eugene Kurtz released BASIC, a programming language that was relatively simple to acquire and use, not least by emerging cohorts of eager programmers. Also crucially, neither Kemeny nor Kurtz copyrighted the language…

Being a well-funded school, one that was eager to develop the most capable students in an age of emerging technology, Lakeside was an early investor in computers for educational purposes. Despite its relative affluence, however, Lakeside could by no means afford the money or space for a massive mainframe, so instead purchased an ASR-33 teletype machine that was connected via a phone line to a PDP-10 computer. For many early technology enthusiasts in the 1970s, a teletype machine was their gateway to the world of computing. Essentially, a teletype was a keyboard-based terminal that enabled two-way communication via a phone line with a distant computer. The user would use the keyboard to input the message. This message would be converted into a punched-tape format and then transmitted to the computer; the computer would reply, the incoming message being printed out to punched tape, which was then converted into plain English. What might seem prehistorically analogue to today's eyes was cutting edge back in Gates' day.

Lakeside's teletype was connected to a remote computer owned by General Electric, who would bill Lakeside according to the amount of time they spent connected. And in those days, computer time didn't come cheap. To fund the new digital outlay, the Lakeside Mothers' Club energized itself and raised $3,000 through a rummage sale, giving the proceeds to Lakeside's newly acquired digital infrastructure. Given what happened to some of Lakeside's future computer users, it was money well spent. For Gates in particular, the system planted, fed and watered seeds of enthusiasm that would change his personal destiny and the destiny of the digital world. In an interview conducted at the National Museum of American History in 1993 Gates acknowledged that there was something almost 'ludicrous today' (Gates 1993) about his early explorations of computer technology because these systems were profoundly underpowered compared to what became available during the 1980s and 1990s, never mind what arrived after those decades. Regarding the teletype print head, for example, Gates explained that it moved at a grinding ten characters per second and didn't have lower-case text functionality. The school computer centre's acquisition of a GE Terminate terminal, therefore – with its blistering 30 characters per second print speed and lower-case letters – represented 'an absolute, incredible breakthrough ... We'd all just sit there and watch it.' (Ibid.).

Gates was clearly hooked, fascinated by the logic, mathematical precision and the seemingly endless possibilities of the system, over which he could exert control and set outcomes through his own powers of logic and invention. He began steeping himself in the core programming languages of the time, especially BASIC. Gates used BASIC to write his very first functioning program – a tic-tac-toe game. He quickly moved forward to a more advanced program, a game in which the user controlled a digital lunar landing, a theme that chimed with Gates' compulsive interest in the US space programme that would put the first humans on the Moon on 20 July 1969. He followed this with a program that enabled the computer to play the board game *Monopoly*. The intellectual fire was lit, and Gates was soon squeezing out every available moment of computer time from Lakeside.

He was not the only one who was hooked. Gates befriended a young man named Paul Allen. Allen was two years older than Gates, but he was a similarly avid technophile and programmer. Like Gates, Allen was obsessed with digital futures, but he was an altogether different character – quieter, more humble, less outgoing, more contemplative, his more internalized character set against Gates' fidgety, hyper-pragmatic and deeply competitive nature. Yet Allen would be every bit as entwined in the foundational story of Microsoft as his more high-profile friend. To give their digital efforts more direction and focus, Gates and Allen paired up with two other techno-kindred spirits – Richard Weiland and Kent Evans – and collectively formed the Lakeside Programmers Group (LPG). The overriding problem immediately faced by LPG was financial. They spent so many hours online that they were quickly working through the initial $3,000 budget. Lakeside had changed its arrangements by signing a new agreement with the Seattle-based firm Computer Center Corporation (CEC), or C-Cubed as it was known, but LPG was soon burning up the hours connecting to a C-Cubed PDP-10, refining their understanding and handling of BASIC, COBOL and FORTRAN along the way.

Gates and the others also quickly discovered they could sneak into corners of the C-Cubed system where they were not supposed to go. This led to Gates' first known 'hack'. As the Lakeside computer-time bills escalated, LPG found a way to access the

Paul Allen and Bill Gates at Lakeside School in 1970, exploring the teletype systems.

C-Cubed accounts, and once in, they modified the record of Lakeside computer time to reduce the bill. The digital trespass was soon discovered, however, and the boys were hauled before the school authorities and punished in the most emotionally targeted way – they were forbidden from using the school computer system for six weeks. But C-Cubed, to its credit, noted emerging talent when it saw it and put it to good use. Being confronted with numerous system crashes among its commercial customers, CEC gave the boys free computer time in return for their deliberate efforts to try to crash the system, identifying the causes and possible rectifications in the process, while also discovering any security weaknesses. This activity took place during the evening and the night-time hours outside the school day, so Gates and the LPG team became untidy, sleepy and red-eyed figures. But for them, the work was absorbing and stimulating, giving them the hours to explore computing in depth. Such was the unwavering passion to discover new insights and optimal solutions that the heavier Allen used to lift the lighter Gates up and drop him into CEC dumpster bins, so Gates could retrieve great armfuls of computer printouts.

Gates remembers this period as a particularly formative time. At CEC Gates and his friends were surrounded by 'some of the great people of early computer days' (Gates 1993). These individuals not only provided Gates and others with inspiration and new ideas, but also practical assistance, lending them technical manuals. Gates remembers that he intellectually hoovered up these manuals with relish, spending hours poring over the instructions and lines of code. For Gates it 'was so exciting to get a little glimpse and beginning to figure out how computers were built, and why they were expensive' (Ibid.). But in his 1993 interview, he also noted the thrill of achieving a certain degree of mastery over a subject at an early age, something he viewed as 'a very positive thing', not least in comparison to the amateur dabblings of most of those around him. The instinct was both educational and competitive. He also noted that while computers were the 'key area of excitement', he was also driven by other academic studies, especially maths.

CEC, therefore, was for Gates a critical immersive step into the computer industry. But for every bright and glowing sun in the early days of the computer industry, there were dozens of short-lived shooting stars that burned out quickly in the unpredictable atmosphere. CEC closed in 1970, just two years after its foundation. The breakdown of the business was instructive to Gates and Allen. They noted that even the most adventurous explorations in tech were useless without solid commercial viability. Gates discovered a silver lining when, along with Evans, he snapped up a large supply of CEC computer tapes from the disbanding C-Cubed. Notably, Gates hid the tapes from the others, but when his secret was discovered he had a major argument with Allen over his actions – such eruptions would become common and ultimately far more severe over the course of their long and complicated relationship.

It is worth pausing the narrative to explore some elements of Gates' developing character in his teenage years. As already noted, he was a true computer obsessive, a trait that for outsiders alternated between being concerning and encouraging, particularly for Gates' parents, who wanted to foster a well-rounded individual. According to some third parties, his truly precocious intellect gave birth to a degree of arrogance – Gates was super smart and he knew it. He debated compulsively over fine points of knowledge or logic, not least with his teachers (throughout his life, Gates has shown little instinctive deference for authority). On one occasion, he literally had a red-faced screaming argument with his physics teacher in front of the class over a matter of science, an altercation that Gates eventually won.

The young Gates also possessed furnace-like levels of energy. Everything had to be done at super speed, deadlines hit right on the very edge of the schedule. Gates began to develop a 'just in time' attitude, with not a moment to be wasted. His intellectual energy was evident despite a frequently appalling diet – in later times, Gates would be seen improvising a meal by licking Tang orange powder drink straight from the palm of his hand, his lower face glowing with synthetic colour. (For reference, Gates' go-to meal throughout his life has been a classic hamburger and fries.) Personal hygiene was frequently neglected, with his hair limp and greasy, dandruff on his shoulders, and body quietly pleading for a shower. His memory, however, was astonishing, bordering on the truly photographic. For example, during his later school years as part of a brief foray into school drama, he memorized a three-page monologue with just a few seconds of studying the pages.

Contemporary students of Gates at Lakeside remember him with a varying orbit of classifications, from obnoxious to inspiring. He certainly seems to have caught attention and was clearly a figure who could divide a room. We should avoid the easy impression, however, that he was merely an oddball geek. Gates was confident and could hold his own with any person put in front of him. He was also something of a thrill seeker. He later became drawn towards fast cars – his first was a red 1970 Mustang bought when he was 16 – and in youth and adulthood he would drive fast and hard, with legal consequences (see below). He also excelled at sports such as waterskiing and skating. Even at physical pursuits, Gates strove to be the best among those around him. He generally succeeded.

The early 1970s brought significant change for the LPG. Allen had branched out and through family contacts was spending more time on computers in various departments of the nearby University of Washington. Gates and the other members of LPG often joined him there in the night-time hours, honing their skills on the university's PDP-10 and PDP-11 computers. Indeed, such was their level of ability that in 1971 came the first business opportunity. The leadership of Information Sciences Inc., a computer timesharing company based in Portland, Oregon, heard of the talented young bunch and approached them to write a payroll programme for one of their clients. Initially, Allen and Weiland decided that the volume of work involved was not great enough for four individuals, so intended to do it on their own. They soon discovered that they needed to pull Gates and Evans back in to handle the workload and the intellectual challenge, especially to tap into Gates' aptitude for elegantly unpacking complex programming tasks. Gates was also valuable for his capacious memory, as the project demanded the quick acquisition of business accounting knowledge: 'I learned about labor reports, taxes, and all sorts of mundane things.' (Gates 1993). Gates' father also assisted by helping the young boys draw up the legal agreement. It was an invaluable foray into the world of digital commerce, bringing funds into LPG (the actual amount is unknown) and providing them with about $10,000 worth of free computing time (Wallace & Erickson 1992: 43). It also gave Gates his first crucial lessons in the art of making a business deal.

By now, Gates saw what began as a hobby as a future career. After graduation, Allen went up to the University of Washington as an undergraduate but maintained his working relationship with the younger boys. For Gates and Allen, the next significant pursuit was a project called 'Traf-O-Data'. Spotting a gap in the market, Gates and Allen developed a program to convert traffic analysis data tapes outputted by local government on-road traffic analysis counters into readable traffic-flow charts. They also hired young computer students from Lakeside to do the time-consuming work of data transcription – they were now starting to understand the relationship between staff and scale. Their ambition for the project soon went up a notch, when they set about trying to build their own traffic analysis computer, based on a new Intel 8008 microprocessor chip. Traf-O-Data would eventually fold when the federal government began providing what were in effect rival services and technologies for free, but by the time it did, Gates and Allen had garnered something in the region of $20,000 from sales (Wallace & Erickson 1992: 45) – serious money in the early 1970s.

Spotting a groundswell of opportunities, Gates and Evans formed the Logic Simulation Company (LSC) alongside LPG, again looking to increase their capacity to take on work by using willing but very low-paid school computer enthusiasts. LSC soon had its first job on the books – developing a new computer class scheduling system for none other than Lakeside school.

On 28 May 1972, Gates faced a psychologically dislocating event, when Evans was killed in a mountain climbing accident. Gates had found a true friend in Evans. They had spent countless hours together working on computers or dreaming of the digital future, mutually energized by technology and its possibilities, as well as just hanging out. In the 2018 Netflix documentary, *Inside Bill's Brain: Decoding Bill Gates*, Gates remembered being deeply unsettled by the suddenness of the event, but we also see his default pragmatism in action: 'It was so unexpected, so unusual. People didn't know what to say to me or to his parents. I sorta thought, hey OK, now I'm going to do these things that we talked about, but I'll do it without Evans.' (Gates 2018).

Gates resumed the scheduling work for Lakeside with Allen's help. When they finally rolled out the program, it worked superbly, so much so that it was still in use in the 1990s. With this proof of delivery, Gates and Allen went on to secure further scheduling-program work with the University of Washington.

Momentum was clearly building behind Gates, his skillset resting on the cutting edge of the new digital horizons. In his senior year at high school, a representative from the mighty TRW, a powerful US corporation with business interests in numerous technological fields, including aerospace, engineering and automotive, contacted Gates. He explained that they needed IT experts to solve problems with a computer system that provided electrical power grid monitoring, and they had heard about the advanced programming skills and problem-solving going on at Lakeside. Jumping at the chance to get involved, Gates and Allen paired up, smartened up, and went for an interview in Vancouver. They got the job, finding professional employment at $165 per week. Lakeside clearly recognized the value of this opportunity and gave Gates permission to miss part of the school year to take on the work.

HARVARD AND BEYOND

In 1973, Gates completed his high school education. Being of exceptional ability and well-connected background, Gates' next stop along the educational highway was Harvard, arguably the most prestigious university in the United States. He had been encouraged to go there by his parents (who doubtless detected that their young son might be deflected down a more commercial route), but Gates was also keen to mix with the finest minds on the planet. Several biographers have noted that he was destined to be disappointed in this regard. For it was Gates who, particularly in the field of computing, was at the top of the game. Such was his intellectual reach that he was allowed to take both undergraduate and graduate courses, excelling at them all, even those in which he had little interest.

Gates took well to college life. He made friends, went to parties, worked hard. He also tried his hand at connecting with female college students, although by some accounts social awkwardness meant that few of these converted into anything more than friendships. One of these friends, Karen Gloyd, remembers him as being somewhat shy and clearly inexperienced with girls (his opening line with her was to ask about her score on the college SAT). But it also seemed that his mind was laser focused on his work and interests, resisting any unnecessary emotional distractions (Wallace & Erickson 1992: 58). This being said, during his later years in college Gates became compulsively involved in the world of college poker playing, putting himself into games in which serious money changed hands. Naturally, Gates was quickly marked down as being one of the more talented players on the circuit.

Academically, Gates remained intellectually unawed by Harvard's students and professors. He did, however, come to the valuable life lesson that he could not be top dog in every field, even his beloved mathematics, a subject in which he came across true luminaries whose abilities even surpassed his own. Nevertheless, one of Gates' notable achievements at Harvard was his finding of a solution to a longstanding mathematics problem related to the maximum number of flips required to sort a pile of variably sized theoretical pancakes in terms of their size, from the smallest on the top to the largest on the bottom. Gates' solution was published in a prestigious journal.

While Gates excelled in his university studies, the tension between throwing himself into academia and pursuing external work remained strong. Indeed, Gates and Allen began to ponder dropping out of university to set up a computer enterprise. Adding to the friction was the fact that they were receiving job offers. One of them came from none other than Honeywell, a huge multinational conglomerate, for whom Gates and Allen both worked as software programmers over the course of a summer. But they dutifully returned to Harvard as summer merged into the fall semester.

Harvard was nonetheless adding kindling to the fire that would become Microsoft, not least in some of the further connections Gates made on campus. One of them was a fellow high achiever called Steve Ballmer, who was studying a degree in applied mathematics and economics (he graduated *magna cum laude* in 1977). Ballmer's room was near Gates', and the two became friends. Ballmer was a socially confident networker, being the manager for the Harvard Crimson football team, a journalist for *The Harvard Advocate* newspaper, and a member of the elite university Fox Club. Ballmer was of a very different psychological make-up to Gates; his drive and confidence would have a special place to play in Gates' future enterprise.

Many hyper-successful entrepreneurs speak of a watershed moment in their careers, a eureka experience in which they both spotted and defined the opportunity that they were compelled to pursue. For Gates and Allen, this came in December 1974, when Allen picked up the January 1975 copy of *Popular Electronics* from a newsstand while walking over to visit Gates. On the front cover, alongside a photograph of a boxy piece of technology, ran the declarative headline: 'World's First Minicomputer to Rival Commercial Models ... ALTAIR 8800'. Magazine in hand, Allen sprinted to Gates to show him the cover and the article, which they rightly saw as proclaiming the first contractions in the birth of genuine personal computing. Their minds racing, the young men saw an opening to provide the machine with a BASIC language interpreter. On 2 January 1975, Allen wrote to the manufacturer, Micro Instrumentation and Telemetry (MITS) in Albuquerque, New Mexico, outlining their proposition, the letter ending on the desk of the larger-than-life (physically and emotionally) former Air Force serviceman Ed Roberts, MITS' boss. The detail of their proposition explained that if MITS paid Gates and Allen $50 per copy of the BASIC they provided, MITS would be able to sell it for $50–100. Roberts saw value both in the proposition and in the prospect of encouraging young entrepreneurship, and he agreed to work with Gates and Allen over the development of BASIC for the Altair 8800.

This agreement was the foundation on which Microsoft was built. Not for nothing is the January 1975 issue of *Popular Electronics* sometimes referred to as the most important publication in the history of the microcomputer.

Gates and Allen now hunkered down into the technical challenge of developing the Altair BASIC to demonstrate to Roberts. There were many hurdles to jump over, not least because Gates and Allen had neither an Altair 8800 computer (the only specimen in existence was at MITS), nor the Intel 8080 CPU it ran on. So before they could get to work on the problem, they also had to reconfigure a PDP-10 computer to mimic the Altair. (Luckily, Allen had previously written an Intel 8008 emulator when he was working on Traf-O-Data, and this could be adapted for the new project.)

By today's standards, the Altair 8800 was wildly basic. For a start, it was initially supplied to buyers as a kit to assemble rather than a ready-to-go computer (later it was offered for an optional fully assembled price). It had only 256 bytes of memory (at the time of writing, 8 gigabytes of working memory is starting to seem pedestrian), although it had 18 external memory slots to take the device up to a whopping 4K. The computer had no screen and no keyboard and was programmed by flicking switches in defined sequences on the front console. Still, at the time it represented the undeniable future of personal computing.

Developing the Altair BASIC proved to be a time-consuming task, and after about four weeks Gates and Allen added a new member to the software team, fellow Harvard student Monte Davidoff. Davidoff had literally overheard Gates and Allen in a university cafeteria mulling over the problem of finding time to write BASIC's mathematics subprogram. Davidoff was already up to speed on such programming and offered his services, which were snapped up.

Together, this three-man team wrote the first BASIC for a microcomputer, completing the task in an intensive eight weeks, the final programme running to 3,200 bytes of data. But they still had to demonstrate that it worked on the Altair. Allen was scheduled to fly out to MITS' rudimentary offices in Albuquerque, to show Roberts what they had done. Famously, on the flight south, Allen suddenly had the gut-punch realization that they had forgotten to write the bootstrap program that would actually tell the Altair how to load up the BASIC. In true seat-of-pants style, Allen wrote the bootstrap on a sheet of paper during the flight. The first opportunity he would have to test that it worked would be in front of a live client.

In the hulking 1.93m (6ft 4in) presence of Roberts at MITS, Allen fed the BASIC into the Altair via a paper tape reader, the youthful entrepreneur waiting for a moment of either triumph or humiliation. After seven minutes of loading time, the machine eventually asked: 'MEMORY SIZE?' Allen inputted '7169'. 'OK', was the reassuring response. Then Allen typed 'PRINT 2+2'. The printer briefly churned out the answer: '4'. There must have been palpable relief in the room. The BASIC was working. MITS had a software solution and Gates and Allen now had a commercial outlet for their programming.

Cutting through the layers of this story, we can observe that Gates alone did not invent the first BASIC for the Altair, although the balance of effort and intellect may have been weighted on his side of the scales. Rather, the BASIC programming in 1975 was a group effort between three men, although Davidoff's contribution would be largely forgotten in later history. But the fact remained that together they had completed the race from brief to delivery. They signed a contract with MITS to supply BASIC and Allen actually went to work for MITS as the director of software development, an interface between MITS and his emerging software company. Gates and Davidoff also moved to New Mexico during the summer semester with another programmer, Chris Larson, to work more closely with MITS. Seeing the snowball starting to roll and gather speed, Gates and Allen also decided to formalize their relationship in a contracted business partnership. They called the new business Micro-Soft.

CHAPTER 2
THE MICROSOFT PHENOMENON

Looking back from our modern computer-saturated age, we need an historical act of imagination to get our heads around what Micro-Soft (in its early hyphenated form) and MITS had done. Together, they were offering an accessible, comprehensible, *personal* computer – the PC – at an affordable price. An August 1975 *Popular Electronics* listing for the Altair 8800 computer was $439 in kit form and $621 assembled, with 4K BASIC for $60 and 8K BASIC for $75. The price model meant that computers came within the financial range of most enthusiasts with a reasonable bank balance, as opposed to the thousands of dollars of outlay for a mainframe corporate machine. The buzz among tech hobbyists was phenomenal and initially transformed the fortunes of MITS, which went from the edge of bankruptcy to a company with 4,000 orders on the books. But here was the problem. Now the issue for MITS was scaling up and meeting the orders from increasingly anxious buyers. Furthermore, the 8080 BASIC, although successfully demonstrated, still needed some polishing before it would ship with the product.

Meanwhile, the partnership that gave birth to Micro-Soft was signed by Gates and Allen on 4 April 1975. There was some contractual wrangling between the two men about profit split. Initially Gates negotiated for a 60/40 split in his favour, and this was later upped to 64/36, with Gates arguing that he had performed a greater share of the development work on BASIC. Allen signed, although later looked back on the agreement with evident discontent, not least because he saw himself as the source of the core idea of marrying the program language with a microprocessor.

If the newly formed Micro-Soft was expecting a sudden inrush of money, however, there would be disappointment after the initial $3,000 signing fee. By the end of 1975, annual revenues for Micro-Soft were just $16,005, despite the fact that the new partners and their early employees were working tirelessly to develop upgraded versions of BASIC. Two big problems soon emerged. First, Gates became aware that computer hobbyist groups and individuals were copying the software and sharing it for free. Among the hobbyist community, there was something of a laissez-faire attitude to copyright infringement, regarding software as something floating in the public domain for common distribution. With the polar opposite belief, Gates was incensed by the illegal copying, especially after all the time and money they had sunk into the project. Clearly gunning for a fight, Gates wrote a now famous 'Open Letter to Hobbyists' and sent it to the influential Homebrew Computer Club, who printed an exact copy in the February 1976 issue of the *Homebrew Computer Club Newsletter*. As we can see in the following extracts, Gates laid his cards clearly and angrily on the table:

> Almost a year ago, Paul Allen and myself, expecting the hobby market to expand, hired Monte Davidoff and developed Altair BASIC. Though the initial work took only two months, the three of us have spent most of the last year documenting, improving and

adding features to BASIC. Now we have 4K, 8K, EXTENDED, ROM and DISK BASIC. The value of the computer time we have used exceeds $40,000.

The feedback we have gotten from the hundreds of people who say they are using BASIC has all been positive. Two surprising things are apparent, however. 1) Most of these 'users' never bought BASIC (less than 10% of all Altair owners have bought BASIC), and 2) The amount of royalties we have received from sales to hobbyists makes the time spent on Altair BASIC worth less than $2 an hour.

Why is this? As the majority of hobbyists must be aware, most of you steal your software. Hardware must be paid for, but software is something to share. Who cares if the people who worked on it get paid?

Is this fair? One thing you don't do by stealing software is get back at MITS for some problem you may have had. MITS doesn't make money selling software. The royalty paid to us, the manual, the tape and the overhead make it a break-even operation. One thing you do do is prevent good software from being written. Who can afford to do professional work for nothing? What hobbyist can put 3-man years into programming, finding all bugs, documenting his product and distribute for free?

[. . .]

What about the guys who re-sell Altair BASIC, aren't they making money on hobby software? Yes, but those who have been reported to us may lose in the end. They are the ones who give hobbyists a bad name, and should be kicked out of any club meeting they show up at.

[. . .]

Nothing would please me more than being able to hire ten programmers and deluge the market with good software.

Bill Gates

General Partner, Micro-Soft

(Gates 1976)

The letter provoked a red-mist backlash from the computer community. Many law-abiding enthusiasts felt they were being shouted at unfairly by a precocious newcomer, while others defended their right to copy software, seeing the practice as akin to that of recording music from the radio.

The reactions augmented wider problems in the relationship between MITS and Micro-Soft. MITS was engaged in a failing struggle to meet orders, and the number of aggrieved customers was stacking up. More problematic for Micro-Soft was that MITS

In the early years of Microsoft, Gates appeared eternally youthful next to Allen, despite only two years' age difference.

had made some commercial decisions it found questionable. They were selling BASIC as a standalone product for $500, a price greater than the computer itself, but for a far lower price users could get BASIC installed on MITS' memory boards. The problem was that the memory boards generally didn't work, thus MITS was unwittingly encouraging customers to copy software to avoid the heavy price of BASIC alone and equally avoid purchasing poor-quality memory boards. Furthermore, MITS was now facing an increasing volume of competition against the Altair. In 1977 alone, three major personal computers were released to the public – the Apple II, Commodore PET and Tandy TRS-80 (the latter sold through the popular RadioShack stores). Collectively these machines became known as the '1977 Trinity'.

It soon became clear to Gates that Micro-Soft had to extract itself from the MITS contract. But this was easier said than done. The contract committed Micro-Soft to a ten-year worldwide exclusivity deal with MITS, meaning that Micro-Soft could not sell its BASIC to anyone else. MITS, by contrast, was legally free to sub-license BASIC to third parties. Thankfully for the future of personal computing, the contract also had some wiggle room. It included the clause: 'The Company (MITS) agrees to use its best efforts to license, promote, and commercialize the Program (BASIC). The Company's failure to use its best efforts ... shall constitute sufficient grounds and reasons to terminate this agreement.' (Quoted in Wallace & Erickson 1992: 92). Here was the loophole Micro-Soft could exploit. And it became increasingly important to do so, as Micro-Soft was bringing out new products, such as a DISK BASIC for a new floppy-disk storage system for the Altair 8800.

It is worth noting the type of company that Micro-Soft was at this point in its history. 'Unconventional' might be the appropriate term. At this stage there was no dedicated Micro-Soft office. Instead, a small band of programmers, including Gates and Allen, worked between a domestic apartment in Albuquerque and the MITS offices. The Micro-Soft personnel were of a definite type – super-bright, rangy, red-eyed programmers, technical whiz kids rather than corporate types, a hiring model that Gates would, over time, struggle to break from. They worked all hours, literally, kept awake by nutritionally poor energy foods and blasting music. Gates was at the centre of it all, his relentless energy rubbing off on those around him. He was intense and argumentative, given to violent emotional fireworks. His combative personality was packaged in a frame that looked way younger than he actually was, so MITS was often treated to the spectacle of what looked like a wiry adolescent boy arguing head-to-head with the full-grown adult Roberts, who found Gates an undeniable handful. Gates could be highly abrasive, not afraid to call ideas or people 'stupid' when he felt they were. Everyone would need to be made of strong stuff to work closely with Gates, and over the subsequent years there would be many casualties.

But no one could argue with Gates' work ethic. He frequently slept in the office, appearing to require just a few hours' sleep in several days to keep him functioning at a high level. (Gates was known for his ability to fall instantly and deeply asleep almost at will, simply pulling a blanket or other covering over his head to summon unconsciousness.) He was also the wellspring of a relentless vision to make Micro-Soft into a global powerhouse company. During the late 1970s, the company's mission statement emerged, variously phrased but summarized as: 'A computer on every desk and in every home, running Microsoft software'. This compact, clear objective became a navigational landmark for the next two decades, coming true in a way even Gates probably did not envisage. The years 1976–77 constituted an important transitional period for Gates and Micro-Soft. Cosmetically but crucially, by late 1976 the name of the company was changed to the punchier Microsoft, creating what would arguably become the most famous brand of the 20th century. In November 1976, Allen left MITS to work full-time for Microsoft and the company grew in outputs and revenues. Around the same time, Microsoft won two big contracts to supply BASIC to US corporate behemoths National Cash Register (NCR) and General Electric, the latter wanting the source code and the former wanting digital cassette-based BASIC for systems based on the new IBM 8080 chip. But the confines of the MITS contract meant Microsoft had to get permission from MITS to pursue further opportunities with BASIC. Gates remembered this time in his interview at the National Museum of American History and also provided a little context to Microsoft's wider activities and personnel:

Well, we knew that MITS was only one company, and we wanted our software to be used on all the machines. And even the original deal we did with MITS talked about our ability to get paid for licenses to other companies. We saw that as Intel was promoting their chip to intelligent terminal makers and other computer makers, that instead of that company writing their own BASIC, we could sell our own BASIC to them for a lot less money. In fact, just do it on a royalty basis. And so we went around convincing

companies like NCR and a lot of the terminal companies that they should make microprocessor-based machines. And so, I was never part of MITS. Paul worked there for about eighteen months and he hired someone else in to take over their software department. And I started hiring other people. In fact, before Paul came back, we had started BASIC for 6800s, 6502s – other chips. We started the FORTRAN compiler. We were talking with Texas Instruments about doing a BASIC for them.
(Gates 1993)

Gates' focus on Microsoft sharpened in January 1977 when he finally gave in to his real motivations and dropped out of Harvard, much to his parents' chagrin. Mary Gates had earlier attempted to head off this decision by arranging for her son to meet with influential entrepreneur and philanthropist Samuel N. Stroum, who was meant to keep Gates on the academic straight and narrow. The plan backfired. Gates so convinced Stroum of his business vision that Stroum actually encouraged Gates to leave Harvard, and indeed later regretted not investing heavily in the Microsoft start-up (Wallace and Erickson 1992: 90). Gates stayed in education a little while longer, but spinning the two plates was unsustainable. In 1984, Gates was interviewed by Jane Pauley on NBC's *Today* programme, in which Pauley asked the still-young entrepreneur whether if he had stayed at Harvard a few more years he would have missed the 'computer revolution'. Gates replied: 'Perhaps. Things move very quickly in this industry and it was really the urgency to get out there and be the first one to put a BASIC on the micro computer that caused me to drop out.' (Gates 1984).

Gates might have been released from Harvard, but there was still the MITS issue to resolve. Things became worse when Roberts began considering selling MITS – and the Microsoft arrangement with it – to the computing company Peripheral Equipment Corporation (PEC). The deal actually went through for $6.5 million on 22 May 1977, PEC rebranding itself Pertec Computer Corporation (PCC). But by this time, Gates and Allen had already filed a legal notice that they were intending to terminate the BASIC licence agreement with MITS. This dispute transferred itself to the new owners, Pertec, who were naturally eager to retain Microsoft under the original restrictive agreement.

The subsequent legal case ran on through 1977, but Pertec may have underestimated the youthful skill of Gates and Microsoft

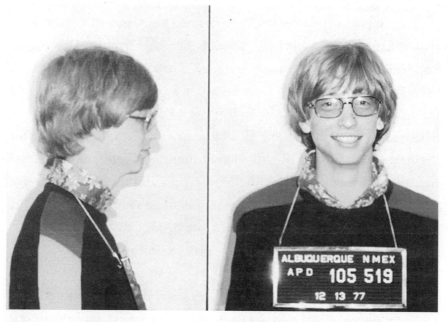

This famous mugshot shows a smiling 21-year-old Bill Gates following his arrest by Albuquerque police for speeding and failure to produce his licence.

(supported legally by Gates' father and his company). A Pertec threat to no longer market BASIC or permit its sale clashed with MITS' clause about fulfilling marketing efforts to promote BASIC, thus the final legal decision fell in favour of Microsoft. Gates and Allen now gained their freedom to sell BASIC to anyone. The brakes had come off.

EXPANSION

The story of Bill Gates and Microsoft from the late 1970s is one of dizzying acceleration. Gates was at the centre of a commercial centrifugal force, spinning ever faster as its products first gained traction and then dominance in the marketplace. Having shaken off the shackles of MITS/Pertec, Microsoft was now roaming free and far.

It is important to remember that at this stage Microsoft was still a languages company, developing programming languages and selling them to third parties. These languages included FORTRAN and COBOL, but BASIC was the commercial driving force, as Gates explained in an interview: 'Yes, this BASIC was the first real piece of software ever written for a PC. And it became for the first generation of PCs, the thing that unlocked the power that was there, because, although some people did machine language programming, 90 per cent of what was done was done in BASIC. And 90 per cent of that was Microsoft BASIC.' (Gates 1993).

MS BASIC became the go-to programming language of the nascent microcomputer industry. It became, for example, the standard language on the TRS-80 personal computer launched in 1977, a system that sold 10,000 units in its first month of sale (which in turn meant 10,000 revenue-earning copies of MS BASIC) and became the top-selling microcomputer until 1982. Its biggest competitor was the Apple II computer, designed and developed under the legendary partnership of Steve Wozniak and Steve Jobs. But although the TRS-80 and Apple II were hardware rivals, Microsoft supplied them both. Wozniak had initially developed a programming language for the Apple II called Integer BASIC, but it didn't incorporate floating-point support (to non-computer specialists, this is an arcane but important technical consideration in representing numbers with a movable decimal point in them). To overcome the problem in timely fashion, Jobs therefore licensed MS BASIC 6502 for the Apple II company. During these early years of both Apple and Microsoft, there was an important co-operative relationship between the two companies, one that gradually moved from programming languages to software applications. Only time and competing priorities would turn the two companies, and Gates and Jobs, into arch commercial rivals.

On a personal level, Gates' principal activity during the late 1970s was hitting the road to sell the MS languages to the Original Equipment Manufacturer (OEM) market. In this arrangement, Microsoft would sell the programming language to a manufacturer to install on their machines and sell on to the customer as part of a complete computer package. Microsoft would make money on the sale of the language licences. Thus bulk-volume deals to OEMs became the beating heart of Microsoft business growth, with Gates working that muscle hard. He was superhumanly tireless in his efforts, criss-crossing the country on flights to visit clients and make the sales. He would operate on an organizational 'just in time' basis, arriving at the airport with only enough bare minutes to reach the aircraft before its doors closed. Note that this practice was not a sign of personal inefficiency or diary disorganization – rather, Gates simply did not want to waste a minute on extraneous tasks, such as hanging around in an airport.

Selling to the OEMs sharpened Gates into a wily negotiator, tough on the terms and hyper-sensitive to any adverse clause a client might be trying to sneak under the radar. Remember that by 1975 Gates was only 20 years old, but still looked much younger. There are accounts of industry professionals scarcely believing that the owner of Microsoft stood in front of them. But intellectually, he was generally the smartest in the room. Not only did he understand computer science to the fullest depth, but he was also extremely shrewd when it came to legal, commercial and contractual considerations.

While Gates had taken the lead as Microsoft's travelling salesman, he was still heavily involved with programming, diligently checking all the code produced by his expanding team of programmers. His hawkish eye for detail was a source of both intimidation and, frequently, annoyance for those who worked under his unsparing spotlight. In the 1986 publication *Programmers at Work*, Susan Lammers (who also became editor-in-chief of Microsoft Press, Microsoft's publishing arm) interviewed Gates about his approach to programming and his role in developing programs at Microsoft. The following extract from his response provides useful context for what was to come, although it is jumping ahead a few years in our narrative:

> I do two key things. One is to choose features to put into programs. To do that, you have to have a reasonable understanding of what's easy and what's not easy to do. You also have to understand what

sort of product 'family' strategy you're pursuing, and what's happening with the hardware.

I also work on the best way to implement that new feature, so that it will be small and fast. For example, I wrote a memo about how to design and implement a feature we used on Excel to make the program recalculate formulas every time the screen changes.

In the first four years of the company, there was no Microsoft program that I wasn't involved in actually writing and designing. In all those initial products, whether it was BASIC, FORTRAN, BASIC 6800 or BASIC 6502, not a line of code went out that I didn't look over. But now we have about 160 programmers, so I mostly do reviews of products and algorithms.

(Lammers 1986: 72)

It is clear that Gates was fundamentally involved in the programming activities of Microsoft, despite other demands on his time. In the first decade of Microsoft, Gates' process involvement graduated from physically writing and designing the code, to evaluating the code written by other programmers, to reviewing the rationale and functionality of the overall products and concepts. In the introduction to Lammers' book, we noted some of the controversies related to Gates' status as a software inventor. In the same year that Lammers' book was published, indeed, one such argument arose.

Programmers at Work was published by Microsoft Press, which was established in 1984 to publish works that would support, either directly or indirectly, the use of Microsoft products. Its first books to hit the shelves were *The Apple Macintosh* by Cary Lu and *Exploring the IBM PC* by Peter Norton. Two years later, the publisher issued the *MS-DOS Technical Reference Encyclopedia*, the first of many editions of a monumental reference work for programmers and computer enthusiasts. (MS-DOS is explained below.) The historical preface to the book included an overview of the development of Standalone Disk BASIC (a version of BASIC running from a floppy drive), focusing on Gates' personal five-day burst of effort in an Albuquerque hotel armed with a pen and a yellow legal pad. Wallace and Erickson in *Hard Drive*, however, argue out that Standalone Disk BASIC was in fact developed by one Marc MacDonald of NRC in 1977, a fact that MacDonald angrily addressed in a letter to Gates after he read the relevant passage in the technical encyclopaedia. As Wallace and Erickson note, subsequent editions of the encyclopaedia were corrected to show MacDonald's efforts more visibly. The 1988 edition, for example, reads as follows:

> Designed and coded by Marc MacDonald, Stand-alone Disk BASIC included a file-management scheme called the FAT, or file allocation table that used a linked list for managing disk files. The FAT, born during one of a series of discussions between MacDonald and Bill Gates, enabled disk-allocation information to be kept in one location, with 'chained' references pointing to the actual storage locations on disk. Fast and flexible, this file-management strategy was later used in a stand-alone version of BASIC for the 8086 chip and eventually, through an operating system named M-DOS, became the basis for the file-handling routines in MS-DOS.
> (Duncan 1988: 8)

To understand this revision, we do not necessarily need to see the original claim as outright falsification. Instead, we might interpret it through the lens of the cult of personality taking root around Gates. This idolization was emerging among Microsoft employees and within the world of computer enthusiasts in the 1970s but spread out through the wider business landscape and indeed to the general public during the 1980s and 1990s. Gates was regarded as the archetype of a new breed of entrepreneur, a human lightning rod for the digital age. When one person gets such laudatory attention, biographical distortions can fuel the compelling narrative. The additional problem is that these distortions might actually distract from the prodigious achievements of the subject.

In early 1979, Microsoft had expanded beyond its mental horizons and physical location in Albuquerque, and thus Gates and Allen relocated the business to Seattle. This move was a big deal for many Microsoft employees. Gates later explained that it 'took a while for me to sell the idea to everybody' (Gates 1993), convincing everyone 'except my secretary [Miriam Lubow]' to make the move. Those who went to Seattle became, in his words, 'the core group'. Furthermore, Seattle provided a fertile location for hiring the additional talent on which Microsoft's future would be built.

Seattle was therefore a judicious choice. Of course, an alternative destination would have been the emergent Silicon Valley in California, the new hub of digital innovation. Doubtless Seattle was attractive on a personal level to Gates by being closer to his family, but the point made about hiring was crucial. Elsewhere, Gates had noted that 'in Silicon Valley everybody changes jobs in 18 months'; by heading for Seattle, Microsoft could build and maintain a stable and talented team. They moved into the Old

National Bank building in Bellevue, settling into its new offices on the eighth floor. Given that Microsoft now had revenues in excess of $1 million, it was able to invest in its own high-end computer system, a powerful DECSYSTEM-20 mainframe costing some $250,000, transforming the company's internal digital capabilities.

Two of the names mentioned in the quotation above deserve some context. For all its growth, at the time of its move to Seattle, Microsoft was still a very small company – just 16 employees at the beginning of 1979. The team included key technical figures such as the programmers Steve Wood and Albert Chu, whose first job together for Microsoft was writing FORTRAN code for the 8080 chip. Indicative of the fact that Gates and Allen were buckling too much responsibility as the company expanded, in 1977, Wood became the Microsoft general manager, taking over from Richard Weiland.

Another key member of the above-mentioned group was Miriam Lubow. Unlike the other Microsoft employees, Lubow did not bring digital skills to the table; in fact, she had never even heard of the concept of 'software'. What she did contribute, by contrast, were superb organizational skills, an understanding of young people, a caring nature and the ability to handle a broad range of administrative duties. She was hired by Wood in 1977 as someone who could work directly with Gates to keep the youthful and often chaotic house in order.

Her first meeting with Gates was both memorable and illustrative. One morning early in her employment, she spotted a young figure dressed in sneakers and denim jeans with dishevelled hair. He walked past her office and went into the nearby computer room, which Wood had told her could only be accessed by authorized personnel. She hurried to find Wood and explained: 'I said, look Steve, this kid runs in there, and he's in that room, and he's working like he owns this place, and Steve says, "Well, you know what, he does. He's your boss. He's the president."' (Quoted in Dudley 2008).

Despite the inauspicious first contact, Lubow became a crucial helpmate to Gates, and indeed to the wider Microsoft team, who came to regard this wise and attentive person as the office 'Mama'. She was especially invaluable to Gates, not only organizing his runaway diary and administrative tasks, but in many ways acting something like a surrogate mother, making sure he was presentable and reasonably well fed, and keeping his mercurial, fast-racing mind grounded in basic health and time-keeping. Her refusal to move to Seattle was a sad loss of support for Gates, although she was replaced by Steve Woods' wife, Marla.

Another key hire just prior to the move to Seattle was the aforementioned 'Steve', by which we mean Gates' old Harvard friend Steve Ballmer. Ballmer was brought in to drive the commercial expansion of the company. Since his days alongside Gates at Harvard, Ballmer had worked for two years as an assistant product manager for Procter & Gamble, before going to Stanford to pursue an MBA. He did not finish the higher degree – Gates lured him away to Microsoft.

Ballmer's arrival was timely. Microsoft's revenues were good and promising steeper growth. The company's client list now included some of the biggest computer and electronics companies in the world – Apple, Commodore, General Electric, Intel, Radio Shack/Tandy and Texas Instruments. Microsoft was also at the beginning of what would be spectacular growth internationally.

One of its biggest opportunities lay in the tech-friendly markets of Japan. Gates and Allen had partnered with an eccentric, electrically energetic character called Kazuhiko 'Kay' Nishi, who headed the ASCII Corporation that he had founded with Keiichiro Tsukamoto in 1977. Nishi was cut from the same cloth as Gates, being computer obsessed, fearless in his ambitions and violently entrepreneurial. Following discussions with Gates, Nishi formed ASCII Microsoft in 1978, effectively acting as Microsoft's agent in Japan. In this role, Nishi was a storming success, making the relationship between Microsoft and ASCII enormously profitable in both directions. He facilitated one of Microsoft's landmark international contracts, supplying software to the Japanese tech giant NEC's PC 8001, essentially Japan's first indigenous microcomputer. This deal gave Microsoft a firm grip over the future growth of personal computing in East Asia. In 1980 alone, ASCII made 1.2 billion yen through licensing Microsoft BASIC, and in return gave Microsoft 40 per cent of their annual revenues.

Nor was it only in Japan where Microsoft was growing internationally. It had forged OEM contracts with the likes of Koninklijke Philips N.V. in the Netherlands, International Computers Limited in the UK and R2E of France, among others. In November 1980, Microsoft signed up a company called Vector International, based in Haasrode, Belgium, as its representative in continental Europe.

The company was going through dizzying levels of change, which suited Gates' high-energy personality down to the ground. Gates wanted Microsoft to be in the driving seat of the personal computing industry. One of the company's early mottoes was the self-confident 'We set the standard.' Gates' approach was not to hang on to the coat-tails of others, but rather to define and develop the industry at a pace that left everyone else desperately trying to catch up, but with a level of innovation that meant that they almost certainly couldn't. To accomplish this, Gates fostered a hyper-fast, long-hours corporate culture, mentally and physically draining on all who worked there. They were not even enjoying high rates of pay. What they did get, in return, was the most intellectually vibrant and cutting-edge workplace in their industry.

As intimidating as Gates could be, he was also something of a hero to many of his employees, who strove to emulate his high-performance attitude. He was also hard-driving in a very literal sense. Around this time, Gates, a man already known for a heavy-footed relationship with the car accelerator, purchased a throaty Porsche 911 sports car and used its 225km/h (140mph) top speed to the maximum. (In fact, at one point he went back to the car dealership to complain that he had only managed to achieve 201km/h/125mph in the car, and therefore it was not as fast as advertised.) One employee remembered that, 'He never went anywhere at less than 80 miles an hour.' (Wallace & Erickson 1992: 130). Marrying Gates' thirst for speed with the Porsche car brought about many near accidents, speeding tickets and even Gates' arrest – he once had to bail himself out of jail for $1,000. But whatever legal frameworks were imposed by society, nothing ever seemed to slow him down.

HEADING FOR THE BIG BLUE

If you thought of computing during the late 1970s and early 1980s, one company above others would take centre stage – International Business Machines (IBM). From the 1960s, IBM had become the powerhouse of global computing, cornering 80 per cent of the US market and 70 per cent of the global market for heavy-lifting mainframes. Such was its gravitational pull in the tech industry that it was also referred to as 'Snow White', with the Seven Dwarfs – Burroughs, UNIVAC, NCR, Control Data Corporation, Honeywell, General Electric and RCA – all mighty companies in themselves, in the shadow of its dominance. It was also known as 'Big Blue'.

Gates knew that if, somehow, Microsoft could connect its software products to the hardware of IBM, it would be a game-changer. But up until the late 1970s, IBM occupied a very different strata of the computer industry and commercial culture to Microsoft. It was focused on big, serious mainframes for big, serious customers. It was deeply corporate, its suit-and-tie personnel working their way up through layers of hierarchy and formalized processes. Microsoft was its antithesis – small, scrappy, informal, disorganized, and focused on the emerging PC market.

But IBM saw that the world was changing. It soon knew the truth – either it too caught the PC wave, or it came late to the party and found itself heading for obsolescence. So, Big Blue decided to create its own PC, development beginning under the top-secret 'Project Chess' programme. As a sign of its break from tradition, rather than develop the PC itself it looked to assemble most of it from third-party suppliers. So, it needed software.

Despite being a trend-setter, Microsoft also needed to innovate, finding new ways to hit the pop-up targets of opportunity as more players piled into the PC market. Intel, for example, was bringing out the new 8086 chip, which offered more speed and greater capacity to run bigger programs. One Microsoft programmer,

Bob O'Rear, developed 8086 BASIC under a simulated 8086 architecture. But to test the software properly, he co-operated with fellow programmer Tim Paterson of the nearby Seattle Computer Products (SCP), a company owned by one Rodney Brock, who also knew Gates. Paterson had built an 8086 CPU, so O'Rear was able to use that hardware to prove his program worked, which it did. The 8086 BASIC subsequently caught a lot of attention in the computer press. The relationship between Microsoft and SCP, however, would not see the two companies ride off into the sunset hand-in-hand...

In further developments, Gates, Allen and others in Microsoft had also spotted the emerging future in software applications, a field in which other companies threatened to steal a march. There were two competing products in particular that got under Gates' skin. The first was VisiCalc (short for 'Visible Calculator'), a spreadsheet financial program developed by engineer Dan Bricklin. VisiCalc ran on the Apple II, indeed was a key asset behind that computer's success. There was also the WordStar word processing program by MicroPro International. This was written for the CP/M operating system created by Gary Kildall of Digital Research Inc., another name and company that would become controversially embroiled in the Microsoft story. March 1980 also saw the release of the opaquely titled SSI*WP word processor by Satellite Software International (SSI); in the early 1980s, this product morphed into the influential WordPerfect.

Galvanized by these software products, and many others, in 1979 Microsoft began focusing intensively on rival applications and formed a Consumer Products Division, headed by Gates' friend Vern Raburn. Gates also hired a marketing director and business manager,

Steve Smith, formerly of Tektronix. Smith quickly proved his worth, working alongside Gates to secure a $150,000 deal with Xerox to provide Standalone Disk BASIC for their new 'Project Surf' PC.

Another area of opportunity for Microsoft lay in developing operating systems, rather than just programming languages. Kildall's CP/M (which stood for Control Program for Microcomputers) was the industry leader in the world of PCs. But not with Apple. Gates and Allen were exercised by the fact that the Apple II had its own 6502 chip and operating system, and thus was unable to accept Microsoft products. Allen, however, had the idea to create a plug-in card through which Apple users could run programs for CP/M. It was called the 'SoftCard' and when it was released in summer 1980, as Microsoft's first foray into hardware, it sold ferociously well. Around this time, Gates also struck a deal with AT&T to license its UNIX operating system, which it sold via Microsoft under the brand name XENIX.

We now return to IBM. It so happened that Mary Gates knew the IBM president, John R. Opel – the two worked together on the board of United Way. Mary discussed her son's work with Opel, who began to sense some possibilities. IBM contacted Gates and, after he had signed IBM's formidable non-disclosure agreement (NDA) he was given insight, as a potential supplier, into 'Project Chess'.

A series of hushed meetings began between the executives of the two companies, the IBM delegation headed by Jack Sams of the innocuously titled Independent Business Unit (IBU). It became evident that Microsoft was well-placed to develop and deliver the languages software, but that IBM also needed an operating system. IBM was initially under the impression that Microsoft held the rights to CP/M. It did not. Nor, crucially, was CP/M currently in a version that would work with the 16-bit Intel 8086 chip IBM was planning to use in the computer.

Gates' connections with Kildall now became key to the IBM deal. Gates and Kildall had a long intellectual and working history, although it had been weakened somewhat in 1979 when Digital Research began packaging a BASIC with its operating system. Wallace and Erickson allege that previously there had been an 'unwritten agreement' that Microsoft would not produce an operating system and Digital Research would not go into languages, an agreement that Kildall reportedly later denied (Wallace & Erickson 1992: 176–78). Had such an agreement existed, it evidently broke down by the turn of the 1980s, but with IBM looking to source an operating system, Gates arranged a meeting between Sams and his team and Kildall.

The events that followed are disputed and cloudy, but also massively consequential for Gates and Microsoft. The core account runs as follows. IBM flew down to Pacific Grove, California, ready to negotiate. Yet Kildall was not there, or perhaps not there initially. Wallace and Erickson describe both sides of the story. Kildall claims he was not there for the initial part of the meeting, but left IBM in the hands of his wife and business partner, Dorothy McEwen, and key members of his team. Kildall joined later and all went well, with an agreement to supply CP/M. Sams, by contrast, claims that Kildall was not present at all at the meeting and that McEwen and her lawyer refused to sign the NDA, so the IBU left empty-handed (Wallace & Erickson 1992: 179–82). What is certain, however, is the ultimate outcome – IBM did not go forward with Digital Research and instead gave the job of developing an IBM operating system to Microsoft.

Now Gates and Allen had to get the job done. They turned once again to Tim Paterson at SCP. Tired of waiting for Digital Research to write an operating system for the 8086 chip, Paterson scripted his own version, which he called 86-QDOS, the 'QDOS' part confessing to a 'Quick and Dirty Operating System'. Gates realized that he could sub-license 86-QDOS (which later became 86-DOS), saving Microsoft long programming hours. In one of those butterfly wings moments in commercial history, Gates asked Sams: 'Do you want to get [QDOS], or do you want me to get it?' Sams apparently replied: 'By all means, you get it.' (Maher 2017). Sams would not know it at the time, but this answer set Gates on the path to becoming the world's richest man.

In the long process of negotiating an agreement between Microsoft and IBM, a pivotal moment came on 30 September 1980. Gates, Ballmer and O'Rear flew down to Boca Raton, Florida, to meet with a panel of IBM executives and to present Microsoft's final report on what they intended to do. Gates realized that this was a pivotal meeting and so upped his sartorial game – he diverted his car during the journey between Miami Airport and the IBM offices to buy a neck-tie, even though this made the Microsoft group late for the meeting.

In an intense boardroom atmosphere, the two companies began thrashing out the deal. In short, Microsoft would supply software and an operating system for the new IBM PC. It was to be a breakneck project, with contract signing in November 1980 but the digital operating system (DOS) and related BASIC supplied in January 1981.

All the work was to be done in cloak-and-dagger fashion, the details known by few inside the companies and even fewer outside. One of those out of the loop was SCP, who knew that

Microsoft had a future PC client, but did not know it was the likes of the mighty IBM, the world's largest computer company. SCP nevertheless signed an agreement to sub-license 86-DOS to Microsoft. Given what Microsoft was working on, the deal was fairly modest. SCP would receive $10,000 on signing the contract, $10,000 for each sub-licence and an extra $5,000 if source code was included (Wallace & Erickson 1992: 194). So, Microsoft would sub-license to IBM and make a fortune, while SCM would recoup just $25,000 on that deal.

The Microsoft/SCM deal was only signed in early January 1981, by which time Gates was feeling the heat over the punishing and ultimately unrealistic schedule. Successive deadlines were missed as the complexities of the project expanded, not least through frequent additional demands from IBM. The number of Microsoft programmers increased to handle the workload, bringing the company to about 70 employees in June 1981. The programmers included the talented Hungarian-American software designer Charles Simonyi, who later became head of Microsoft's Applications Group.

Despite the pursuit of secrecy, details of the IBM program progressively trickled out, including to Rod Brock, who had an additional reason to be aggrieved with Gates as Tim Paterson had been lured away from SCM for Microsoft. Matters between the two companies came to a head in July 1981, when Gates managed to persuade Brock to sell 86-DOS to Microsoft for $50,000, with the agreement that Microsoft would then sub-license DOS back to SCP and provide updated versions. Brock signed, mindful that Microsoft was now in a better position to take the DOS forward, but it would prove to be a fateful signing on his part.

On 12 August 1981, IBM finally unveiled its Personal Computer (as it was unimaginatively named), running on what was called PC-DOS 1.0. Note that Microsoft, who called the software MS-DOS, was still able to market the DOS to other OEMs. To IBM, however, Microsoft also provided the BASIC, COBOL and PASCAL languages and some other software (such as the game Microsoft Adventure). MS-DOS was only just at the beginning of a long and at times troubled evolution, but it was clear from the outset that Gates, Allen and the team had secured an extraordinary deal. IBM was quickly selling about 40,000 units a month of its PC, each running the licensed Microsoft software. At the same time, Microsoft licensed MS-DOS to some 50 other hardware manufacturers in the first 16 months of its release. This torrent of sales quickly translated to the balance sheet. By the end of 1981, Microsoft had revenues of $16 million; in 1982, that figure rose to $24.5 million; in 1983, $50 million; in 1984, $97.4 million, by which time the company had more than 600 employees (the company was compelled to move to larger premises near Lake Washington in the autumn of 1981).

Growth also brought restructuring. On 25 June 1981, Microsoft became a private corporation in the State of Washington, meaning that employees and investors could become shareholders in a company that clearly had a bright future. Gates took pole position on the leadership board as president and chairman of the company, with Allen acting as executive vice president. The three leading figures of the company – Gates, Allen and Ballmer – took 51, 30 and 7.8 per cent of the company respectively. Allen's contribution to Microsoft was seminal, but it was clear who was holding the reins.

It is common for entrepreneurs heading young, successful businesses to redefine their role in their own company during a growth phase. Yet unwillingness to relinquish a death grip on the day-to-day running often runs headlong into the reality that the company they founded is now too big to be managed effectively by one person, however powerful their personality. Gates was confronted with this dynamic. Gates had great strengths in tech development and product sales, but some of the more quotidian and formulaic (but important) aspects of running a business, such as disciplined bookkeeping, allegedly ran beneath his radar. Thus in the summer of 1982, Ballmer persuaded Gates to take a new company president, hiring James Towne, a former senior executive from Tektronix.

Towne was on all kinds of levels a very different creature to Gates. He was nearly double Gates' age and had a wife and children. They had completely different work rhythms – Towne was in the office early and left at a reasonable time, whereas Gates would often come in later but work almost through the night. It seemed that from the outset the two were set on a collision course. Reportedly, most difficult for Towne to manage was the fact that night-owls Gates and Ballmer would often meet and make decisions in the small hours of the morning, at which time Towne was at home tucked up with wife and family. Towne left in 1983 and Gates once more stepped back into his shoes.

It was not only Towne with whom Gates was having a difficult relationship. The working atmosphere between him and Allen was also often strained. Gates and Allen went back to the very beginning of the Microsoft story and beyond. In the following passage from a 1993 interview, Gates explained how he and

Allen shared the initial excitement at making an impact in the digital arena:

> The vision is really that in the information age that the microprocessor-based machine, the PC, along with great software, can become sort of the ultimate tool dealing with not just text, but numbers and pictures, and eventually, even difficult things like motion video. And that is something that when Paul and I would go around speaking about computers, we would always say that there were no limits. We used to call it the 'MiPs to the Moon' speech. ['MiPs' refers to Million Instructions Per Second, an approximate measurement of computing power.] That performance would be unbounded and that all of these incredible things would happen. We were never too specific about exactly when various things would happen. And, of course, when we went back to our business we had to decide what our priorities were. But, the frontiers were sort of wide open. It was that sense of excitement that we really wanted to spark in everybody else wherever we went.

Gates' affection and high regard for Allen is clear in this passage. But, for some significant periods, there were profound conflicts between the two. Allen himself explained the nature of these conflicts in his insightful 2011 memoir, *Idea Man: A Memoir by the Co-founder of Microsoft*. In the book, Allen self-observes his resentment at Gates' insistence on the company ownership split weighted heavily in his favour. But in the early 1980s, everything changed. In 1982, Allen became ill on a business trip. Subsequent medical investigation revealed that he had Stage 1-A Hodgkin's lymphoma, a form of blood cancer. It was treatable, for now, but

Allen suddenly had other priorities in life than wrestling with Gates and Microsoft.

Following diagnosis of his illness, the division between the two men actually seemed to intensify. Allen recounts how in December 1982 he overheard Gates and Ballmer speaking irritably in Gates' office. Allen alleges they were talking about what they saw as problems with Allen's productive input and how 'they might dilute my Microsoft equity by issuing options to themselves and other shareholders. It was clear that they'd been thinking about this for some time. Unable to stand it any longer, I burst in on them and shouted, "This is unbelievable! It shows your true character, once and for all." I was speaking to both of them, but staring straight at Bill. Caught red-handed, they were struck dumb. Before they could respond, I turned on my heel and left.' (Allen 2012: n.p.). Allen judged this as 'mercenary opportunism, plain and simple' (Ibid.). In 1983, Allen would leave Microsoft, but he ensured that he went on his own terms. Gates offered to buy Allen's Microsoft stock for $5 a share, but Allen refused and insisted on $10. Gates would not pay this, so Allen left the company retaining his stock, a decision that ultimately led to Allen being a multi-billionaire and one of the world's richest people. He went on to have a stunning and innovative career beyond Microsoft but died in 2018 of non-Hodgkin's lymphoma.

Allen's book would stretch taut any lingering bonds of friendship with Gates, but the roots of old friendship went deep and never completely broke. In an interview with *The Wall Street Journal* in March 2011, Gates explained of this time: 'While my recollection of many of these events may differ from Paul's, I value his friendship and the important contributions he made to the world of technology and at Microsoft.' (Rusche 2011). There would, in time, be a reconciliation between the two men, although many years would go by before that came to pass. But looking back, their early relationship was forged in hothouse days, fuelled by youthful passion and doubtless the mental side-effects of epic hours of work. Gates was certainly a man whose focus on maximizing efficiency and optimizing outputs could express itself in ruthlessness. But what is equally clear is that unblinking hard stare would be needed in the years to come.

CHAPTER 3
FROM WORD TO WINDOWS

On 13 March 1986, Microsoft went public, its stock opening at $25.75 and selling ferociously to an expectant market. A year later, the shares were worth more than $90, making Gates, who owned 49 per cent of Microsoft stock, officially a billionaire. Clearly, Microsoft was on the up, but Gates had actually been wary about the implications of the Initial Public Offering (IPO). His concern was that many shareholding members of staff would become instant millionaires, or at least very wealthy, and thus the corporate culture would suddenly become less motivated, losing its competitive edge. Also of note, the IPO revealed Gates' salary as $133,000, which was way less that was typically paid to the CEO of a major corporation.

Whatever was driving Gates, it wasn't his personal bank balance. Nevertheless, in 1987, at the age of just 31, Bill Gates took his place in the billionaire club. (Just to give this number an inflationary context, $1.00 in 1987 would be worth $2.66 in 2023.) Not only had he achieved fantastic personal wealth, but he was at that point in history the youngest billionaire ever.

Gates had certainly packed a lot into his 31 years, but this was just the beginning of his climb up the financial ladder. Between 1995 and 2017, with the exception of the years 2010–13, Bill Gates was the richest person on the planet. (He was finally knocked off the top spot in 2018 by Jeff Bezos.) He was also becoming one of the most influential. Through Microsoft, Gates was almost literally fulfilling his vision of a computer in every home and every office around the developed world, running Microsoft software.

We have journeyed across Gates' childhood and youth and the foundational years of Microsoft. Our continuing narrative will take us through the 1980s and 1990s. These were the defining decades in Gates' commercial career, those in which Microsoft achieved global dominance in computer software. For Gates, this meant a shift from being lauded as a highly successful young businessman to the equivalent of entrepreneurial deification. The scale of his accomplishment and public profile was perfectly captured by the cover of *Time* magazine on 5 June 1995, the year in which Gates' company released the game-changing Windows 95 software. The cover illustration showed a confident-looking Bill Gates holding up his hand, a lightning-flash graphic added between his thumb and forefinger. This image, alongside the headline 'Master of the Universe', treated Gates akin to a digital god, as if Gates had internalized the act of divine creation embodied in Michelangelo's painting *The Creation of Adam*. The cover tagline, however, also slipped in a warning: 'Having conquered the world's computers, Bill Gates takes aim at banks, phone companies, even Hollywood. He's in the fight of this life.' Although the cover might seem sensationalist or sycophantic, in 1995, Gates' software was almost effectively the digital gateway for the intellectual and commercial economy of the planet. But as the last sentence implied, the future would be no easy ride, even for someone of Gates' capabilities.

THE SOFTWARE EXPLOSION

At the beginning of the 1980s, MS-DOS and Microsoft languages were doing roaring good business. But Gates, his eyes constantly scanning the horizon for both threats and opportunities, saw that the future lay in software applications – programs that got stuff done. It also lay with a different sort of customer. Gates no longer wanted to train his sights mainly on the hard-core techies, but instead sought to expand into the furthest reaches of the general population. As he explained to one programmer, he wanted to make software so accessible that even his mother could use it (Wallace & Erickson 1993: 208–09).

What appeared to be something of a benevolent streak was counterbalanced by continuing ruthlessness towards the competition. Gates' desire was not simply success in a crowded field. Rather, he wanted to run his competitors out of business or at least consign them to also-rans. Immediate targets included Digital Research (which was still producing the rival CP/M operating system), VisiCorp (manufacturer of the VisiCalc spreadsheet), MicroPro (manufacturer of WordStar) and Corel (WordPerfect). Gates would soon have others on the list. There was also the matter of Apple, which had gone public in 1980 to great fanfare, offering an attractive and increasingly modish alternative to the Microsoft digital landscape.

At Microsoft, Gates tasked Charles Simonyi, of the Xerox Palo Alto research lab, to lead the advance into applications. Simonyi was a founder member of the Xerox Palo Alto Research Center (PARC), a digital research and development company based in Palo Alto, California. He was fully on board with Gates' vision – he predicted wildly transformed revenues for Microsoft's future in the applications market. But there were many hurdles to cross before the money began rolling in.

The key software battlegrounds of this period were spreadsheets and word processing applications. Microsoft's first big splash in this domain came with the release of its spreadsheet software Multiplan, released in 1982. Multiplan was designed to fight it out with VisiCalc, which at that time was selling well on IBM computers. But it turned out to be the wrong fight. In January 1983, Lotus 1-2-3, a well-conceived and effective spreadsheet program by Lotus Development Corporation, hit the shelves and the press with much fanfare. The problem for Microsoft was that Lotus 1-2-3 was regarded as much better than Multiplan. It was more intuitive, more capable, and it ran faster, being designed purely for the IBM PC and not, like the Microsoft product, for multiple hardware platforms. It was by now clear that the IBM PC was going to become the industry-standard personal computer, with surging start-ups such as Compaq Computing Corporation legally reverse-engineering PC-compatible computers from 1983, with astonishing success.

Much of this was still good for Microsoft's bottom line. It meant that MS-DOS found new legions of loyal customers. By the mid-1980s, MS-DOS was the standard non-Apple system; CP/M was effectively gone, drowned in the Microsoft floodwaters. Multiplan, furthermore, was not by any means a complete commercial flop – it sold more than 1,000,000 copies. But it was eventually outperformed in the market by Lotus 1-2-3, an outcome that reportedly made Bill Gates furious and intent on reasserting Microsoft's dominance. It would be some years before Microsoft produced a world-beating spreadsheet program that consigned

Lotus 1-2-3 to history. But in the early 1980s, it had a different software ace up its sleeve – Microsoft Word.

Word had been developed by a Microsoft team headed by Simonyi and programmer Richard Brodie. It was publicly demonstrated in the spring of 1983 before being released on 25 October 1983. A note about branding is important here. It was originally planned to call the software 'Multi-Tool Word', a member of a Multi-Tool software family, which included Multiplan. But Rowland Hanson, Microsoft's capable new corporate communications manager, suggested renaming it to link both product and company in a more direct, memorable way. Hence Microsoft Word was born.

Bill Gates, CEO of Microsoft, seen here in 1985. He was on an upward trajectory – two years after this photograph, he became a billionaire.

In a 1993 interview, Gates explained that with Word he wanted to do something that was 'very forward looking' (Gates 1993). Building on the recent hire of Simonyi, the Microsoft team focused intensely on the graphical interface, plus the interaction of that interface with the new generation of laser printers coming over the horizon. 'So we designed something whose underlying structure was ready for the graphical world.' (Ibid.). On-screen, Word would show text features such as italic and bold, all within a precision layout, and even though the screen resolution itself might be underpowered, the print-out from a laser printer would be crisp and would also reflect what was shown on-screen.

Gates knew what would be the critical factor behind Word's success. It was a WYSIWYG ('What You See Is What You Get') program, meaning that the document that appeared on the screen would look the same once it was printed out. It also had drop-down menus integrated with mouse operation plus the ability to create style sheets. Users could work on multiple documents at the same time. Word 2.0, released in 1985, also added word count and spell check functions.

Word was not born perfectly formed. Thousands of working hours and frequent updated versions would be needed to get the program hitting all the key performance indicators. Furthermore, the early Word had to compete against two popular products, WordPerfect and WordStar. Word found a solid handhold in the market during the 1980s, but it would not be until 1989–90 that Microsoft sprinted to the head of the pack. In 1989, Microsoft released Word for Windows. Then on 22 May 1990, Microsoft unleashed Windows 3.0, an operating system with next-generation improvements in look, speed, features and memory management.

It was a massive success, with 4 million copies sold in the first year and rave reviews. Ramming home the advantage, that same year Microsoft brought out WinWord 1.1 for Windows 3.0. The fusion of Word and Windows, combined with the increasing power, utility and user-friendliness of the Word program, transformed the word processing market. Both WordStar and WordPerfect were unavailable in versions for Windows until 1991, by which time Microsoft had become the market leader through an aggressive sales and distribution strategy, such as including a free trial disk of the product with computer magazines.

Excel was another of what would come to be regarded as Microsoft's 'killer apps', with flexible and intuitive functionality and an emerging 'family feel' alongside other Microsoft productivity applications. It was Microsoft's answer to Lotus 1-2-3, plus a pre-emptive strike against a new Lotus spreadsheet in development, known as Jazz, a program in which Apple had invested. Excel was launched on 2 May 1985 at the Pierre Hotel, New York City. Gates personally led the demo and did so in the presence of Steve Jobs – Excel had also been designed to run on Apple computers. (Also in 1985, Microsoft released Word for Mac, further cementing the Macintosh/Microsoft fusion as a go-to option for businesses.) As an indicator of Gates' heightened state of mind during this event, exacerbated by the crash of the Excel demo during a run-through, he announced Excel in a notably dishevelled state, having been up for most of the night, neither showering nor shaving before he took to the stage. But the demo went well on the day, plus Excel would receive excellent press reviews and rampant sales figures. Excel would eventually, like Word, surpass all the competition, and over the next half decade it effectively killed off Lotus 1-2-3 and Jazz.

Two years after the release of Excel, in 1987, Microsoft spotted another opportunity in the office productivity software market. Specifically, it was a presentation program developed by engineers Robert Gaskins and Dennis Austin of a Silicon Valley start-up called Forethought Inc. It was called PowerPoint. Having caught the attention of John Sculley, the new CEO of Apple, PowerPoint was announced as an Apple product at the Personal Computer Forum in Phoenix in February 1987 and began shipping the following April.

According to the account of Jeff Raikes, head of marketing for Microsoft's Applications Division, Gates was initially unimpressed by PowerPoint when Raikes suggested presentation software as a market opportunity. In a Microsoft Developer Network video entitled 'The History of Microsoft – The Jeff Raikes Story: Part Two', Raikes explained how he had to move Gates to see his position:

> I thought, 'software to do overheads—that's a great idea.' I came back to see Bill. I said, 'Bill, I think we really ought to do this;' and Bill said, 'No, no, no, no, no, that's just a feature of Microsoft Word, just put it into Word.' ... And I kept saying, 'Bill, no, it's not just a feature of Microsoft Word, it's a whole genre of how people do these presentations.' And, to his credit, he listened to me and ultimately allowed me to go forward and ... buy this company in Silicon Valley called Forethought, for the product known as PowerPoint.
> (Raikes 2010)

Microsoft purchased PowerPoint for $14 million, the value of the acquisition reflecting the importance Microsoft came to attach to presentation software. PowerPoint was officially released by Microsoft on 22 May 1990, co-ordinating with the release of Windows 3.0. Like Excel and Word, it would go on to become one of Microsoft's most popular office applications. In what was clearly a busy year, in October 1990 Microsoft released MS Office, bundling three of its most popular productivity programs – Word, Excel and PowerPoint – into one compelling package for both Apple and PC users. Over time, various other Microsoft products would be bundled into Office (such as the Outlook email software) to increase its desirability, giving Office more than 80 per cent market share in the email and authoring software market for much of the 2000s, although in recent years (as Office 365) it has lost a significant share to competition from cloud services such as Google Workspace.

THE GUI – FROM XEROX PARC TO WINDOWS 1.0

Today, the computer mouse is almost as familiar as the human hand that uses it. Back in the 1980s, however, the mouse was a bold new development in the human/computer interface. Although precursors dated back to the 1940s, the first practical mouse devices emerged during the 1960s. But during the 1970s, the true pioneer of the mouse device for the PC was Xerox PARC. PARC was genuinely one of the founding fathers of modern computing, not only for the computer mouse, but also for its conceptual corollary, the graphical user interface (GUI), which would become fundamental to the story of both Bill Gates and Microsoft.

Unless you have lived a life of exquisite isolation, you will be familiar with the GUI. It is the landscape of interactive icons, often accompanied with audio inputs, that enables us to navigate intuitively around the computer and to operate programs with nothing more than the click of a mouse button. In 1973, Xerox was the first company to introduce a PC – the Xerox Alto – that had a GUI and a crude accompanying mouse. But the first company to capitalize on the GUI commercially and to explore its full potential was Apple.

Intellectual liaison between Xerox PARC and Apple began in 1979, and in 1983 Apple released the Apple Lisa computer, complete with GUI and mouse. This was superseded by the faster, cheaper Macintosh computer. The Macintosh was every bit as impactful as anything emerging from Microsoft. It was first promoted on 22 January 1984 through one of the most memorable moments in the history of visual advertising. An Apple television commercial, directed by Ridley Scott and entitled '1984', was screened during Super Bowl XVIII to an audience of millions of Americans. In the figure of an athletic young woman hurling a throwing hammer into a grey screen indoctrinating a mute audience, Apple represented the shattering of old norms and the liberation of those looking for new horizons in computing.

Gates and Microsoft were integral elements in the development of the Macintosh, as Gates himself here explains:

> The really unique thing we got into was when Steve Jobs came up and talked about what he was doing with the Macintosh. He solicited us to write a family of applications for that machine. And because of our background in looking at what Xerox had done with graphics interface, we were very excited about this design. [...] instead of really attacking 1-2-3 just at the DOS level, we

decided we would focus on the graphical version and do the work on Macintosh and Windows and sort of be a generation ahead if we were right about graphical interface. So Microsoft worked very closely with the early Macintosh team. We were their testing group. They had no testers. We helped shape the features of the machine.

(Gates 1993)

Gates was evidently an enthusiastic endorser of the Macintosh, but within this quotation we can also see it as something of a testbed for a Microsoft GUI. The implications of that would soon arise.

Winding back a little, in October 1983, all was well between Bill Gates and Steve Jobs, and Apple and Microsoft. During that month, Jobs hosted a high-profile sales conference for Apple staff. Attempting to give the event extra levity and sparkle, Jobs at one point took the role of a question master for the coyly titled 'Macintosh Software Dating Game', which featured three special guests: Frank Gibbons of Software Publishing Co., Mitch Kapor of Lotus, and none other than Bill Gates of Microsoft. In front of Apple staff and the world's media, Gates was famously effusive about Microsoft's relationship with Apple; when asked to introduce himself to the audience, Gates included the snippet of information that half of Microsoft's revenue would come from Apple. Jobs also asked him if the Macintosh computer represented a new industry standard: 'Well to create a new standard it takes something that's not just a little bit different. It takes something that's really new and really captures people's imagination. And the Macintosh, of all the machines I've ever seen, is the only one that meets that standard.' (Gates 1983).

Gates was clearly an Apple believer. He even participated in an internal promotional video for Apple in 1983, in which he expressed his approval of the forthcoming Macintosh, saying: 'It's a great machine. It's a step forward in terms of the way it uses graphics; and the speed. This is a machine that a lot of people are going to be able to afford.' (Huddleston 2020). If Gates was aware that the Apple computer was, to some degree, a potential threat to Microsoft more than a commercial partner, he was hiding it well. Indeed, in a 26 November 1984 *BusinessWeek* article, Gates proclaimed that 'the next generation of interesting software will be done on the Macintosh, not the IBM PC'.

Even as the Macintosh computers were flying off the shelves, Microsoft was already hard at work on its own GUI. This was initially called the 'Interface Manager'. Gates was ambitious about the Microsoft GUI. His ultimate goal was not only to make the Microsoft GUI the industry standard in the PC market, but also to package that GUI with multiple compatible and appealing Microsoft software applications. Thus Microsoft could build a dual path to market dominance, winning people over to the core GUI while at the same time using that GUI to promote adoption of Microsoft applications. Soon the Interface Manager received an important name change, again from the fertile brain of Rowland Hanson. It was decided to call the new software 'Windows'.

Gates already had a head start in the development of Windows by having two former PARC employees now on his payroll – Simonyi and Scott MacGregor. As momentum built behind the Microsoft project, Gates soon attracted others from PARC.

Windows progressively took shape, but as it did so Microsoft set itself on a potential collision course not only with Apple, but also with IBM, at that time Microsoft's largest trading partner. By 1984, IBM was looking to reclaim some of its independence from Microsoft in the software market and had decided to build its own operating interface. This was branded as TopView and was announced in August 1984, with shipping beginning in March 1985.

TopView was not a GUI – it was rather a multi-tasking shell – but it was an alternative to Windows, and potentially a powerful one in the hands of IBM. The emergence of TopView initially galvanized Gates to push ahead with Windows at full steam. He signed agreements with 24 major new computer companies, including companies that would become virtual household names, such as Compaq and Hewlett-Packard. The agreements committed the companies to adopting or supporting the forthcoming Microsoft Windows.

Microsoft was also now competing in the GUI domain not only with the giants Apple and IBM, but also with a new company called VisiCorp, who had produced its own GUI called Visi On. In a clear pushback against Microsoft, IBM then signed an agreement with VisiCorp to be a Visi On distributor, even though IBM was developing TopView. Add the fact that yet another company, Quarterdeck, was also producing a GUI and it was clear that Gates and Microsoft were on a crowded racetrack, jostling for pole position.

A key priority for Gates in this race was to steal VisiCorp's thunder by announcing the impending arrival of Windows before the official release of Visi On. So on the morning of 10 November 1983, at the Helmsley Palace Hotel in New York City, Gates gave the press an excited vision of what was coming down the road from Microsoft. In the presentation of 'Windows

1.0', he promised great things: compatibility with all MS-DOS applications; multiple software applications running at the same time; switching between software applications using the mouse; adoption of Windows by 90 per cent of all IBM-type computers. The scarcely hidden message in this address was that if you didn't wait for Windows, the rival GUIs might be obsolete from the very moment you bought them.

But Windows simply wasn't ready, and wouldn't be ready for much time to come. When Gates unveiled Windows 1.0, most people in the room would have been expecting a release a few weeks or at most a few months later. As it turned out, Windows didn't even go to manufacturing until 1985, with Gates and Microsoft frequently embarrassed in the intervening months after promising, and failing, to hit successive release dates.

Biographical accounts of Bill Gates' contribution to the development of Windows are somewhat guarded. While Gates was not working as a frontline programmer any more, he absolutely was involved in defining the functionality and features that would go into the software. He was vigorously observant of every technical decision and, according to insider reports, frequently changed the parameters and goal posts, reportedly leading to exhausted frustration in the programmers, who found themselves working interminable hours on constantly shifting sands. According to Wallace and Erickson, Gates and Ballmer, who was put in charge of the Systems Software Division, constantly underestimated the time it took to complete core tasks, simultaneously taking a dim view of any human factors that interfered with the speed of development while micromanaging at every opportunity (Wallace & Erickson 1993: 301). Jennifer Edstrom and Marlin Eller's *Barbarians Led*

By Bill Gates: Microsoft from the Inside also describes how, in August 1984, Gates suddenly decided that Windows had to be redesigned so that it could work without relying on a mouse, just using the keyboard, a diktat that further ate into development time (Edstrom & Eller 1998: 59–60). (Their chapter on the development of Windows is darkly titled 'Death March', suggesting the visceral experience of those involved in the project.) Gates was in constant arguments with MacGregor, who headed the group in charge of Windows. Eventually he had had enough, and left Microsoft entirely before Windows hit the shelves.

The Microsoft programming team may well have been the computing equivalent of Top Gun fighter pilots, but they still could not deliver the impossible. The rolling delivery promises made by Microsoft led to press critics coining the term 'vapourware', meaning software that was announced but had yet to materialize in reality. Over time, the principle behind vapourware would come to have legal significance, as whether it was delivered or not, the announcement of a future program could have major market impact on competitors. Many OEMs, for example, would hold out for the Microsoft offering in the future rather than buy a competing product that was available in the here and now, the company wanting to avoid a purchase that became instantly obsolete the moment Microsoft's product finally met the release date.

Windows 1.0 finally went on sale in November 1985, following Gates' theatrical announcement of it at the COMDEX computer fair in Las Vegas (the very place where he had first witnessed a demonstration of Visi On). Windows was absolutely a work in progress. It had problems with software compatibility and performance, and placed high demands on system requirements.

Plus, as the press were quick to point out, as a GUI it compared unfavourably with the slicker offering from Apple. But it at least put Microsoft on the GUI pathway.

And yet here lay the root of a further problem Gates would have to negotiate. Another criticism levelled at Microsoft was that its operating systems sector and its applications division fell under the same corporate umbrella. This meant that Microsoft applications programmers had a competitive advantage over external companies developing software for Microsoft platforms, by being able to share information more quickly and readily between the application and platform sides of the equation. Gates publicly stated that there was in effect an 'invisible wall' separating the two parts of the company, although several Microsoft insiders subsequently questioned whether this wall was as impervious as Gates suggested. It would not be the first time that Microsoft and Gates would be accused of using its corporate muscle and advantage to take the lead in the industry.

IBM AND APPLE

For Bill Gates in the second half of the 1980s, IBM represented both a problem and an opportunity. The opportunity lay in IBM's scale, brand and market presence, the very reasons why Microsoft had hitched a ride with Big Blue in the first place. The problem was that the tracks the two companies had been running on were showing signs of divergence, not least through the competition emerging between TopView and Windows.

A more serious faultline in the Microsoft/IBM relationship, however, developed from an initial collaboration on a new IBM operating system, known as OS/2, which was intended to be released with the next generation of IBM computer, the Personal System/2 (PS/2). OS/2 was essentially intended to be the next generation of DOS. IBM also began developing a future version of OS/2 called 'Presentation Manager' – this would be IBM's unilateral attempt at a GUI, independent of Microsoft. (By this time, the shift of focus to GUIs meant that IBM's TopView was fading from view.)

Here, there was much to concern Gates. Presentation Manager would, in effect, be a direct competitor to Windows, which was an operating system IBM had already said it didn't want to support. So in December 1986, Gates and Microsoft negotiated with IBM to share development of the OS/2 Presentation Manager, Gates being keen to ensure that he rode the right horse into the future. This move put MS Windows in a particularly awkward position, not least because OS/2 Presentation Manager would not support Windows applications. Microsoft's involvement in the development of OS/2 Presentation Manager proved nearly unworkable at a corporate level, but Gates threw his weight behind the IBM/Microsoft relationship. For a time, it even looked like Windows might be killed off (Ballmer positively advocated that move), even though many Microsoft programmers actually felt that OS/2 was going to be a dud.

Ultimately, they were proved right. OS/2 was released in December 1987 followed by Presentation Manager in October 1988. Neither of them would set the market aflame, having their fair share of technical and marketing problems. What they did reignite, however, was Microsoft Windows, despite IBM suggesting to Microsoft that it restrain the development of Windows to keep OS/2 centre stage. Gates gave a telling video interview in 1987 in which he was asked directly about how heavily Microsoft was reliant upon IBM's business. His reply is worth watching, not least for the hesitancy of an ambitious man choosing his words guardedly:

> Well, everyone relies on their best customer quite a bit. IBM worked with us in the creation of MS-DOS and that became a very important product for us. And now we've worked together on OS/2, which is the latest generation operating system. It is critical to us to continue to be innovative in a way that our customers find important and IBM's at the top of that list. So, I think we'd do fine without them but it would certainly be a big loss. [...] We were in this business a long time before IBM got involved and in fact we helped them make the crucial designs that helped them make the original PC and so all our eggs aren't in one basket.
> (Gates 1987)

Everything changed in 1988. During that year, a small internal Microsoft team, led by programmer Dave Weiss, unilaterally began reviving and redesigning Windows. Weiss had been a real catch for Microsoft. He had formerly worked for Dynamical Systems Research (DSR) in Oakland, California, a company with its own GUI that essentially did everything that TopView did, but with greater speed and reduced demands on memory. When Microsoft became aware of what DSR was doing, it sent a team to investigate. They were impressed by what they saw, so in June 1986, Microsoft bought the DSR company and its team. Weiss and programmer Murray Sargent redeveloped it to run in 'protected mode', which basically meant that multiple applications could run simultaneously without crashing the computer. With other improvements, the new version of Windows would do everything that OS/2 Presentation Manager could do, just better, and with full support for Windows DOS applications.

In the summer of 1988, Gates and his senior management team received a presentation of the new Windows led by Weiss. Microsoft had already upped its game with Windows through the announcement of Windows 2.0 in April 1987, offering significant enhancements to the user interface (especially through having overlapping rather than tiled windows), improved keyboard shortcuts and better memory management. But the version of Windows demonstrated by Weiss was in a different ball park. Plus, it was going to crush IBM's GUI offerings. Gates, always ready to embrace innovation wherever it led, was not dissuaded by this fact. Ballmer asked Gates in the meeting: 'What do we tell IBM?' Gates replied, 'I don't know Steve, that's your problem.' (Edstrom & Eller 1998: 93).

Microsoft, therefore, picked up the Windows ball again and ran with it. IBM soon got wind of the development and were not pleased. IBM effectively told Gates to kill off Windows and Gates apparently seemed to comply – even the press reported stories that OS/2 Presentation Manager was going to sideline Windows. But it was not to be. Windows 3.0 was released on 22 May 1990 and took off like a rocket. It sold 2 million licences in six months and its successor, Windows 3.01, sold 10 million licences. It established Windows as *the* platform for personal computing. Microsoft continued to work on OS/2 Presentation Manager for some time yet, but the writing was on the wall. Microsoft would eventually take the OS/2 3.0 variant and use it to build the Windows NT GUI for workstations and servers, which was released in July 1993. By this time, the Microsoft/IBM collaboration was effectively dead, but Microsoft was by now in a different league altogether.

A BITE OF THE APPLE

We have already seen the feel-good factor that existed between Apple and Microsoft in the early 1980s. But the mood would get progressively darker. In November 1983, Gates had announced Windows 1.0. Like the Macintosh, Windows was a GUI and mouse set-up. According to insider accounts, Steve Jobs exploded in anger when he saw the Microsoft offering, incensed at what he regarded as Microsoft's copying of fundamental elements of the Apple GUI and packaging them in Windows. It led to a high-stakes confrontation between Jobs and Gates (it would not be the last). According to an inside account, told in Walter Isaacson's excellent *Steve Jobs: The Exclusive Biography*, Jobs lay into Gates in front of ten Apple employees: 'You're ripping us off! I trusted you, and now you're stealing from us!' According to Andy Herzfeld, one of the Apple programmers present at the meeting, Gates then delivered a cool, now legendary, counterpoint: 'Well, Steve, I think there's more than one way of looking at it. I think it's more like we both had this rich neighbor named Xerox and I broke into his house to steal the TV set and found out that you had already stolen it.' Gates' course was now set: 'We are doing Windows. We're betting our company on graphical interfaces.' (Isaacson 2011: p.163).

It was a strong retort. Plus, Gates had a contractual advantage on his side. The original contract signed between Apple and Microsoft in 1981 included a clause that prohibited Microsoft from releasing software based on mouse interaction until a year after Apple had released the Macintosh computer. To nail this down temporally, the contract therefore stipulated the date as September 1983, a year after the expected Mac release date. However, the Macintosh release date slipped to 24 January 1984, but that movement in the calendar was not reflected in an amended contract. Thus even though Windows stole a march on the Mac, Microsoft was still legally within its rights to do so. Furthermore, Gates threatened to withdraw Word and Excel from the Mac if Apple went ahead with the action. Given that these two programs were hot-sellers for a struggling Apple, they didn't want to go down this road.

In an effort to clarify relationships between Apple and Microsoft, Gates and Sculley, the new Apple chairman, signed an agreement on 22 November 1985. The opening of the agreement gave the context of the dispute and a mea culpa from Microsoft:

> The parties have a long history of cooperation and trust and wish to maintain that mutually beneficial relationship. However, a dispute has arisen concerning the ownership of and possible copyright infringement as to certain visual displays generated by several Microsoft software products. [...] For purposes of resolving this dispute and in consideration of the license grant from Apple described in section 2 below, Microsoft acknowledges that the visual displays in the above-listed Microsoft programs are derivative works of the visual displays generated by Apple's Lisa and Macintosh graphic user interface programs.
> (Apple-Microsoft 1985)

This paragraph might seem to prelude an agreement weighted in favour of Apple, but it went on to give a concession to Gates' position that would have fateful consequences for Apple in the long term:

> A. Grant. Apple hereby grants to Microsoft a non-exclusive, worldwide, royalty-free, perpetual, non-transferable license to use these derivative works in present and future software programs and to license them to and through third parties for use in their software programs. This license shall not include new software programs written by Microsoft which are similar in function to Microsoft Excel and are offered to the public prior to October 1, 1986. As a condition to this license, Microsoft shall cause its visual copyright notice to appear in its products which use visual displays licensed hereunder.
> (Ibid.)

This clause meant that, beyond certain date and product limitations, Gates and Microsoft were free legally to take Windows anywhere. At the same time, the agreement went on to compel Apple to back down from developing an operating language they called MacBASIC, which would effectively be a competitor to Microsoft's BASIC. Also, in exchange, 'Microsoft hereby grants to Apple a nonexclusive, worldwide, royalty-free, perpetual, nontransferable license to use any new visual displays created by Microsoft during a period of five years from the date of this agreement as part of its Microsoft Windows retail software product in software programs and to license them to and through third parties for use in their software programs.' (Ibid.).

But the friction between Microsoft and Apple over competing GUIs was not ultimately salved by contractual framing. In March 1988, problems resurfaced as Apple once again threatened to sue Microsoft over the introduction of Windows 2.03 (Hewlett-Packard was also a target of Apple legal action, related to its introduction of the NewWave GUI). Apple's contention was that Windows was violating copyright through features that Apple saw as clear derivatives from its Lisa and Macintosh interfaces, including core elements such as overlapping application windows and pull-down menus. At the same time, the legal challenge threw up potential for Apple to take action against IBM's Presentation Manager.

This time, the *Apple Computer, Inc. v. Microsoft Corporation*, 35 F.3d 1435, would not be resolved without legal judgement. The opening paragraph of the 1994 judgement on the case set the scene:

Lisa and Macintosh are Apple computers. Each has a graphical user interface ('GUI') which Apple Computer, Inc. registered for copyright as an audiovisual work. Both GUIs were developed as a user-friendly way for ordinary mortals to communicate with the Apple computer; the Lisa Desktop and the Macintosh Finder1 are based on a desktop metaphor with windows, icons and pull-down menus which can be manipulated on the screen with a hand-held device called a mouse. When Microsoft Corporation released Windows 1.0, having a similar GUI, Apple complained. As a result, the two agreed to a license giving Microsoft the right to use and sub-license derivative works generated by Windows 1.0 in present and future products. Microsoft released Windows 2.03

and later, Windows 3.0; its licensee, Hewlett-Packard Company (HP), introduced NewWave 1.0 and later, NewWave 3.0, which run in conjunction with Windows to make IBM-compatible computers easier to use. Apple believed that these versions exceed the license, make Windows more 'Mac-like,' and infringe its copyright. This action followed.

(US Court of Appeals, Ninth Circuit 1994)

Gates was shocked by the action, not least because he had met with John Sculley, the Apple CEO, the day before the filing and Sculley made no mention of what was in the pipeline (Wallace & Erickson 1993: 352). Gates responded publicly in an interview with the *San Jose Mercury News*, the tone of his comments clearly indicating that he was stung by the claims:

> He never mentioned it to me ... not one word. So I told people at first, when the rumors started, that it wasn't true. Then we found out they'd called all these reporters and sent them all a copy of the lawsuit. This was a massive [public relations] attack... We're confused. I'm not kidding. I've been involved in a lot of lawsuits and every lawsuit I've been in, I've thought, 'I hope we're OK.' But not this one. You have to wonder – if they're rational people – what are they thinking... Apple is using the press to send a message. The suit is supposed to strike fear into people's hearts and make them think that Apple invented this stuff and not Xerox.
>
> (Quoted in Wallace & Erickson 1993: 352)

The *San Jose Mercury News* interview was just the beginning of Gates' pushback against Apple in the press. He sought to depict the battle as an unjustifiable attack on the ability of software companies to develop GUIs of their own. In the 28 March 1998 issue of *InfoWorld: The PC News Weekly*, an article by Nick Arnett and Scott Palmer entitled 'Gates Challenges Apple Copyright Claims, Citing Licensing Agreement' saw Gates defend Microsoft by pointing to the wording of the 1985 agreement. Gates argued:

> We're saying that these graphic interface techniques, the ideas, are not copyrightable. [...] Even if this stuff originated with Apple and it were copyrightable, and even if people didn't own their own applications when they write with various techniques, there is still this license [...] There is nothing that has happened in Windows to move it closer than that. [...] We're not trying to claim some of the credit, but yes, the original applications were written by us – take various techniques, like the zooming and window drop-down, and the way the controls work, stuff like that [...] We had more people working on Macintosh software than Apple did, so we had some influence.
>
> (Arnett & Palmer 1988)

With Gates convinced of his company's position, it was clear that Apple and Microsoft were heading into battle. This was big news in the computing and business world at the time – the first ten pages of the quoted *InfoWorld* magazine were largely devoted to the story, with concerns that the scrap would affect all developers of windows-type GUIs. There was even an article analyzing whether the Apple fight would cloud the future of IBM's Presentation Manager.

The legal case between Apple and Microsoft would play out over six years. Much would change over that period. Xerox piled into the case, arguing that it, rather than Apple, was the true aggrieved party in the case, although in 1990 this position was legally dismissed. Meanwhile, Microsoft's business was powering on. The release of Windows 3.0 added further fuel to the fire, with Apple adding additional claims to its case, which was certainly not restraining Gates' ambitions. 'We are going to be aggressive about doing new things for Windows,' he said in September 1990 (Johnston 1990).

Apple Computer, Inc. v. Microsoft Corporation and Hewlett-Packard Co. was not finally settled until 1994, having passed through district court to the US Court of Appeals for the Ninth Circuit. The court ruled in favour of Microsoft, stating that 'Apple cannot get patent-like protection for the idea of a graphical user interface, or the idea of a desktop metaphor [...] almost all the similarities [between the two systems] spring either from the license or from basic ideas and their obvious expression ... illicit copying could occur only if the works as a whole are virtually identical.' (US Court of Appeals, Ninth Circuit 1994).

While Apple and Microsoft had been fighting it out, times had changed. Apple's commercial fortunes were steadily becoming more constrained, while Microsoft was achieving epic results and an ever-tightening grip over the computing market. Microsoft was certainly not the little guy any more. In 1990, the company had revenues of $1.18 billion. It had 5,635 employees on the payroll, most working from a huge new-build campus-style headquarters in Redmond, Washington, where the company moved in February 1986. The company's physical expansion would continue apace, with further offices dotted throughout the United States and abroad.

The personal relationship between Gates and Jobs would be mercurial and complex, occasionally combative and even disdainful. But it is evident that there were sinewy connections binding the two companies together. Jumping ahead a little, in August 1997, with Jobs back in the company (he officially became Apple CEO the following month), Apple had fallen on hard times and was facing outright bankruptcy. At that point, Gates stepped in with a $150 million investment in Apple that essentially saved the company. The cover of *Time* magazine showed an image of Steve Jobs crouched and speaking into a cell phone quoting the Apple executive: 'Bill, thank you. The world's a better place.' Not everyone felt so warm toward Gates; when Jobs announced the investment at the Macworld Boston Conference, the audience booed when Gates made an appearance via satellite.

But the synergy between the two companies and the two men, although brittle at times, was on balance productive. In 2007, a decade after the Microsoft investment, Gates and Jobs appeared on stage for a lengthy joint interview at the D5 Conference, where they reflected on their relationship. Thinking back on the 1997 rescue, Jobs reflected:

Apple didn't have to beat Microsoft. Apple had to remember who Apple was because they'd forgotten who Apple was. [...] To me, it was pretty essential to break that paradigm. And it was also important that, you know, Microsoft was the biggest software developer outside of Apple developing for the Mac. So it was just

crazy what was happening at that time. And Apple was very weak and so I called Bill up and we tried to patch things up.
(Jobs and Gates 2007)

Gates also recognized that reconnecting with Apple was to their mutual benefit. 'That's worked out very well. In fact, every couple years or so, there's been something new that we've been able to do on the Mac and it's been a great business for us.' (Ibid.).

Steve Jobs died from cancer just four years after this event, on 5 October 2011. By this time, Apple had returned to be a powerhouse in digital devices, with Microsoft being left in its wake in key arenas, as we shall see in the next chapter. But Gates was 'truly saddened' by the passing of a man he described as a 'colleague, competitor, and friend'. Through his blog, he gave a simple, moving tribute:

> Steve and I first met nearly 30 years ago, and have been colleagues, competitors and friends over the course of more than half our lives. The world rarely sees someone who has had the profound impact Steve has had, the effects of which will be felt for many generations to come. For those of us lucky enough to get to work with him, it's been an insanely great honor. I will miss Steve immensely.
> (Gates 2011)

Together, Bill Gates and Steve Jobs had reshaped the world. Their battle over GUIs remains one of the great legal and intellectual struggles of the digital age, and one in which Gates eventually emerged as victor. As the next chapter will explore, however, the 1990s and the 2000s also saw Gates take what would be his greatest commercial defeats, as the computing landscape shifted beneath his feet.

CHAPTER 4
NEW TIMES, HARDER TIMES

In the mid-1990s, the future was looking very different to the past through which Microsoft had climbed to success. What was different this time was the arrival of something very new, potentially revolutionary, in the digital landscape. Unlike applications software, operating systems, programming languages, hardware or indeed any of the tools Microsoft had used to build its position, this new phenomenon was not owned by anyone. It was not centralized or circumscribed. You could not buy it. And yet it promised one of the greatest exponential transformations in the history of the human interface with technology. Everything would change – knowledge, commerce, information, data, social interactions, politics. The internet was arriving.

Paradoxically, Bill Gates' relationship to the internet during the 1990s appears to the outsider as both misdirected and central. Microsoft had by this decade achieved unrivalled global dominance in PC software. That position would maintain its upward direction throughout the decade, ultimately ensuring that most of the computerized world would, to some degree, encounter the internet through a Microsoft interface at some level. But as we shall see, the arrival of the internet was a prelude to Microsoft's slip from 'setting the standard', a slip that accelerated into something of a headlong fall during the 2000s. From the first decade of the new millennium, other companies would in many ways become the driving force behind the digital future. As Microsoft had been, these companies would go from scrappy start-ups to global powerhouses and household names, the likes of Facebook, Amazon, Apple, Google and YouTube. Microsoft would remain absolutely central to computing, but in key areas it lagged behind the curve, resulting in some of the biggest failures in the company's history, although these are balanced to a certain extent by hitting the mark on other targets.

But the period from 1995 to 2008, the focus of this chapter, also marked a profound change in personal direction for Bill Gates, not least in relation to the company he founded. We see his gradual disengagement from the practicalities of running Microsoft, leading to his official step-down from day-to-day involvement in the company in 2008 (although he would remain active on the Microsoft board until 2020).

We can read this move from several perspectives. One is to see it as part of Gates' long-term vision to move into the next phase of working life, focused squarely on what would turn out to be deeply impactful works in philanthropy and international development. We could also see it as a by-product of Gates' advancing age; after all, by the year 2000 he had been running flat out for Microsoft for more than two decades. Finally, we might also read his slow exit from the company as an acceptance that the technical outlook he possessed that took Microsoft to global dominance might not actually serve him as well in the shapeshifting digital future. Of course, all three could, to varying degrees, be true simultaneously.

THE INTERNET AGE

The year 1995 was pivotal for both Microsoft and for Bill Gates. In fact, in some ways it was one of the most significant years in the history of personal computing. During the first half of the decade, Microsoft had enthroned itself not just as a giant in the computing industry, but almost as the branded embodiment of global computing itself. By the end of 1992, 44 per cent of the whole software market was in Microsoft's hands. In 1994, Microsoft revenues had hit $4.6 billion, the phenomenal earnings pushed skywards by established products and numerous new introductions – multimedia products such as Encarta and Bookshelf, plus applications for making music, creating art, education, managing finances, developing databases and much more. In July 1993, it brought out a fresh GUI for corporate applications, Windows NT, which would be highly successful, sitting alongside the integrated networking software Windows for Workgroups. Not for nothing was Microsoft named the '1993 Most Innovative Company Operating in the U.S.' by *Fortune* magazine.

Gates' position and stature was also changing during the 1990s. By 1995, he was not 'merely' one of history's great entrepreneurial success stories, with the personal wealth of $20 billion. He was also, in effect, one of the most influential human beings on the planet, given his status in relation to the digital economy. As we shall see, this was something of a mixed blessing, especially when it came to governmental attention. But his achievements were now recognized at the highest levels. In 1993, President George H.W. Bush awarded Gates the National Medal of Technology and Innovation at a White House Rose Garden ceremony, acknowledging Gates 'for his early vision of universal computing at home and in the office; for his technical and business management skills in creating a worldwide technology company; and for his contribution to the development of the personal computing industry.'

But Gates has never been an individual to bathe in complacency. Indeed, by the mid-1990s, he was frantically attempting to reorientate Microsoft to the impact of the internet on both the world and his business. A seminal document signposting his shift in thinking was an internal memo written by Gates and sent to Microsoft staff on 26 May 1995. It was headed 'Internet Tidal Wave' and consisted of Gates' lengthy exposition about the technicalities and impact of the emerging internet. The opening paragraphs of the document clearly threw down the gauntlet for Microsoft:

> The Internet is at the forefront of all of this and developments on the Internet over the next several years will set the course of our industry for a long time to come. Perhaps you have already seen memos from me or others here about the importance of the Internet. I have gone through several stages of increasing my views of its importance. Now I assign the Internet the highest level of importance. In this memo I want to make clear that our focus on the Internet is crucial to every part of our business. The Internet is the most important single development to come along since the IBM PC was introduced in 1981. It is even more important than the arrival of the graphical user interface (GUI).
> (Gates 1995)

So, the internet was now firmly the future for Microsoft. The problem was that Gates and Microsoft were already coming slightly late to the party.

Although military and governmental precursors to the internet dated back to the 1960s, the World Wide Web as we know it arrived in 1991, courtesy of work performed by the English computer scientist Tim Berners-Lee at the European particle physics laboratory the *Conseil Européen pour la Recherche Nucléaire* (CERN). By 1993, it was clear that the marriage between the apparently indefinite expansion of PC adoption and internet networking and search capabilities was going to be transformational, as reflected in the Gates memo. But by the time Gates wrote it, others had already taken the lead.

In 1992, two programmers from the University of Illinois at Urbana-Champaign's National Center for Supercomputing Applications (NCSA) – Marc Andreesen and Eric Bina – decided

The launch of Windows 95 was accompanied by a $300 million global marketing push. Here Bill Gates promotes the operating system at the 'Inside Track 95' event in the National Exhibition Centre, Birmingham, UK.

to create a pleasantly accessible web browser, simple enough for all to use. With parallels to Microsoft's early hunger for being faster than the rest, Andreesen and Bina accomplished their development challenge in just eight weeks. At the end, they released the Mosaic browser software, which as an NCSA product was distributed free to anyone who wanted to download it. There were other browsers at this time, but Mosaic established a surging lead – it was running at 50,000 downloads per month by mid-1994. (To give this figure some context, remember that only 2 per cent of the US population of 263 million had access to the internet in 1994.)

Then in April 1994, Andreesen partnered with tech executive Jim Clark and founded a company called Netscape, which in turn engineered a new browser called Navigator. Even more so than Mosaic, Navigator was the web browser the world was crying out for. It was fully compatible with the latest trends in website multimedia, including images, video and audio. The PC-owning world rushed to adopt it and Netscape first created a virtuous circle of growth – the more internet users there were with Navigator, the more that companies and individuals created websites to fuel their interests, and the more people downloaded Navigator. Navigator's adoption rates rivalled anything achieved by Microsoft software. It grabbed 70 per cent of the browser market by 1995, with annual revenues of $45 million. Andreesen, fresh to the billionaire's club, even featured on the cover of *Time* magazine in February 1996. Bill Gates and Steve Jobs were now not the only digital superstars.

One aspect of the future was clear to Gates – Netscape was a curve-ball competitor that had to be either absorbed or crushed. Microsoft began developing its own internet browser, Internet Explorer, in the summer of 1994. To accelerate the project timeline,

Microsoft reached a licensing deal with Spyglass Inc., an internet software company that had been licensed by the University of Illinois to develop and sell a commercial version of Mosaic. Internet Explorer was scheduled for release in 1995 alongside the unveiling of another crucial Microsoft product, the revolutionary new GUI called Windows 95.

The fight was now on. Gates wanted to let the world know that Microsoft was opening the throttles in what became known as the 'browser wars'. The memo 'Internet Tidal Wave' was just one signal of Gates' intent. Although it was technically an internal document, it was leaked in full to the press, which published it and agonized over its details and implications. According to a source quoted by James Wallace: 'Frankly, I think Bill was getting tired of all the stories about Netscape. I don't know who actually leaked the memo, but it was done with Bill's knowledge.' (Wallace 1997: n.p.).

We should contextualize the 'Internet Tidal Wave' document by saying that Gates saw the internet's future in a far wider context than just doing some academic research on a PC. As he had always done, Gates was hard at work attempting to divine the future, exemplified in a speech that he gave at the 1994 COMDEX conference:

There is no slowing as we look at the next decade in terms of the processor speed or memory size or storage capabilities of these systems. It's really up to us to think, how do we want to take advantage of that? Of course, at the center of this will be the idea of digital convergence. That is, taking all the information, books, catalogs, shopping approaches, professional advice, art, movies, and taking those things in their digital form, ones and zeroes, and being able to provide them on demand on a device looking like a TV, a small device you carry around or what the PC will evolve into. All of these form factors will count. But we'll need to have a common architecture so we can take all the authoring, the work done to prepare this media and make it easily available to people using these different devices. So this is what we're reading about all the time, with all the different stories. The communications companies have to think about this because it is their future. Media companies, from TV to cable, to Hollywood studios, need to get involved because it is their future. The consumer electronics industry is coming into this and will need to be one of the ones building these devices. Certainly, for the PC industry, this is what it's all about. Lots of advances, lots of things that we can draw on to have growth in years ahead. So even at 40 million units a year we still have lots of frontiers to conquer and lots of impact.

Gates was clearly prescient about the direction of computing. In November 1995, Gates further clarified his thoughts about the digital future with the publication of his first book, *The Road Ahead*. Gates is not unusual in being an entrepreneur who, once success has provided stability and credibility, puts pen to paper. But as we shall see, Gates is one of the more prolific of these writers. His publications, however, are not self-aggrandizing 'how I made it narratives', but rather discrete windows into technical, commercial, scientific or development projects that matter to Gates. In all his books, the subject matter, not himself, takes centre stage.

The Road Ahead was a co-author project, written between Gates, Microsoft programmer and executive Nathan Myhrvold and Pulitzer prize-winning writer and entrepreneur Peter Rinearson. Although published in 1995, the book quickly went through substantial revisions to republish in October 1996, with an additional 20,000 words of content, suggestive of the fast pace of change in the technology industry. The book was essentially Gates' manifesto about how computers and the internet were going to shape the future. In particular, the internet was going to give users unprecedented access to information, entertainment, services and shopping, any time they wanted it. 'What sets this period in history apart is the ability to manipulate and change information, and the speed at which we can handle information. Almost all information will be digital. Once digital information is stored, anybody with permission and access can recall, compare, and refashion it.' (Gates 1996: n.p.). He unreservedly called this change a 'revolution' and was energized by it: 'I'm still thrilled by the feeling that I'm catching that first revealing hint of revolutionary possibilities.' (Ibid.). There was much work to do, however, before Microsoft could fully ride the internet wave.

WINDOWS 95

In 1995, Microsoft might have been struggling to catch up in the browser wars, but in other areas of digital development its power was almost unchallenged. And it was about to get bigger. On 24 August 1995, Microsoft launched Windows 95 to the public. Here was the next-generation GUI. Its improvements over previous versions of Windows were legion. It had a dramatically enhanced interface, the user clicking on a large 'Start' button in the bottom-left corner to access most files and applications, but with a new taskbar at the bottom giving quick start routes to frequently accessed programs.

The system featured a new Windows Explorer file manager and Control Panel, and included an enhanced plug-and-play capability for hardware interactions. There were improvements to the file naming systems, file-sharing protocols and memory management, plus the overall package was much better for those who wanted their computer for gaming and multimedia applications.

The launch of Windows 95 rested atop one of the biggest marketing efforts in computing history. The lead-up to the official launch event on 24 August included weeks of high-profile media coverage and advertising, the leading TV advert using The Rolling Stones' 'Start Me Up' as its soundtrack, a creative decision that cost Microsoft millions of dollars in licensing. There was even a comedic 'cyber sitcom' episode featuring *Friends* superstars Jennifer Aniston and Matthew Perry visiting the Microsoft headquarters and fumbling around with Windows 95. Gates personally gave 29 interviews on major networks in the week before the launch.

The actual launch event for Windows 95 took place in a large tent constructed on the grounds of the Microsoft headquarters in Redmond, Washington State. In a party-like atmosphere, 2,500 of the world's most influential journalists, business executives and other movers and shakers had gathered, representing about 30 countries. The event was also broadcast around the world via satellite. (Fulfilling Gates' vision for instant access to information, the entire event can be watched online for free – see https://www.youtube.com/watch?v=_JzfROUDsK0&t=4765s). None other than the comedian/*Tonight* show legend Jay Leno had been recruited as host for the spectacle, bringing a polished and confident humour that helped to smooth over some of the awkwardly choreographed comedy and interaction between him and Gates. But whatever the merits of the staging, there was no doubt that by the end of 24 August 1995, almost the entire developed world knew about the launch of Windows 95.

The initial buying of Windows 95 was physically riotous in stores globally. The Associated Press ran a sceptical headline: 'Windows 95 Sales Mania on Day One, But How Long Will It Last?' (https://apnews.com/article/5abfa8c012e765b3c68c4569cdf68584) As it turned out, sales would be strong and durable, both off the shelf and through the OEM market. By early September 1995, it had sold 1.63 million copies, and then 40 million copies in the first year.

But the issue of Microsoft's position in the browser market remained unresolved. Navigator was still leader of the pack. Microsoft's answer to Navigator was Internet Explorer, released at the same time as Windows 95 but as part of the Microsoft Windows 95 Plus! pack. Microsoft had signed a licensing deal with Spyglass, using the Mosaic source code and offering a quarterly payment plus a percentage of royalties on the sale of each copy of Internet Explorer. But that relationship soon started to fracture as Microsoft took new directions to market. First, Microsoft started issuing Internet Explorer free with NT (and thereby distributing without paying a royalty), a move that prompted Spyglass to sue; this legal case was finally resolved in 1997 with Microsoft paying Spyglass $8 million to buy out future royalties. Then Internet Explorer 2.0 was released as a free download.

This was just the beginning of Microsoft's unwavering efforts to compete with and then dominate Navigator. With its deep pockets, Microsoft was able to improve Internet Explorer progressively, with Internet Explorer 3.0 (August 1996) and 4.0 (September 1997) matching then exceeding Navigator in many features.

Internet Explorer was eventually integrated into Windows 95 and its successors as standard – if you bought the interface, you got the browser. Microsoft also began flexing its buyer muscles, persuading OEMs to install Internet Explorer as the default, at the expense of Navigator.

By attacking the issue on multiple fronts, Microsoft won the day. By the end of the 1990s, Netscape as a company and Navigator as a browser were on the ropes, their markets and revenues collapsing. What had once been the most successful internet browser had effectively disappeared by 2007–08 (it had less than 1 per cent market share in 2006). On 15 July 2003, Netscape was disbanded by its then owner, Time Warner. Gates had won the browser war. But there was a cost.

GATES ON THE STAND

The 1990s saw the birth of a protracted and, for Microsoft, potentially dangerous legal challenge. Unlike its fight against Apple and others, this time it came directly from the US government. Although the case of the United States vs. Microsoft was fundamentally a battle between a corporation and the US polity, to a large degree Gates himself would be on trial. Government commissioners and prosecutors would rigorously interrogate Gates' entire approach to doing business and how he handled his leading role in Microsoft attaining market dominance. Gates pushed back hard, seeing the government onslaught on Microsoft as tantamount to an attack on capitalism itself.

The seed of the legal conflict was planted in the early 1990s, when the Federal Trade Commission (FTC) began to investigate claims, brought by several software developers, that Microsoft was abusing its market power in relation to rival operating systems and GUIs, smothering competition and free enterprise, particularly in regard to application software and word processors. They questioned the supposed impermeability of Microsoft's 'invisible wall' between applications and operating systems divisions. The FTC also began assessing the larger question: had Microsoft, including through its collaboration with IBM, achieved genuine monopolistic power over the American and the global computer industry?

The investigation gathered pace in 1992–93, as the FTC hunkered down in its fact-finding, gathering many thousands of pages of testimony, evidence, and analysis. The FTC's Bureau of Competition believed it had developed a strong antitrust case against Microsoft. Yet on two occasions, the FTC took a vote on whether to implement legal action against Microsoft and on both occasions the four commissioners found themselves deadlocked with a 2–2 vote for and against. Normally there would be five commissioners voting, which would have avoided any potential deadlock, but one of the commissioners had to recuse himself because he had inherited a trust fund that included Microsoft stock.

That might have been the end of the matter, but there was an unforeseen escalation when the US government's Department of Justice (DOJ) instead took up the case. Many at Microsoft, indeed many in the press, felt that there was a degree of political motivation in the attack, elements of the US government keen to hobble a company it saw as too influential. When he heard the news that the DOJ was taking over, Gates was reportedly incandescent; according to one eyewitness he was literally hurling objects around the room (Wallace 1997: n.p.). In Gates' view, Microsoft's ascendancy was simply the product of relentless innovation and canny business strategy. In June 1993, Gates gave an interview for *Time* magazine, and spelled out his defence clearly, directly attacking his accusers:

> Lotus lost ground because it was very late in catching the two biggest technology waves: the Macintosh and Windows. Borland International is too distracted with its bad merger with Ashton-Tate. Philippe Kahn [chairman of Borland International, a software company] is good at playing the saxophone and sailing, but he's not good at making money. WordPerfect is truly a one-product company. Our most successful software is for the Macintosh. We have a much higher market share on the Mac than anywhere else. How does Apple help us? Well, they sue us in court. In the future, maybe our competitors will decide to become more competent. (Wallace 1997: n.p.)

Gates was clearly not bowing down.

Regardless of Gates' public protestations, the DOJ investigations went ahead. The scale of the case involved an interminable period of legal preparation on both sides, one that cost Microsoft millions of dollars in legal fees. But eventually it reached court on 18 May 1998 at the US District Court for the District of Columbia in the presence of Judge Thomas Penfield Jackson and no fewer than 20 US state Attorneys General.

The particulars of the DOJ's case focused on two main narratives. First, that Microsoft's tactics aggressively and unfairly prevented Netscape's Navigator from holding on to its market share. Second, the DOJ alleged that Microsoft used similar tactics to undermine Sun Microsystems' sale of JAVA, a new object-oriented programming language that was a superb web editing tool but which threatened Microsoft because it could run on almost any computer, not just those with Windows installed.

The legal proceedings in the case of *United States of America* (plus the *State of New York*) *vs Microsoft Corporation* were punishingly long and factually complex, and are beyond quick summation here. But Microsoft faced a rapid-fire range of accusations, from deliberately configuring Windows to make it difficult for rival software to be installed and run, to withholding important technical information from competitors, to effectively coercing computer manufacturers to exclude other products to retain the Microsoft relationship. But the overarching thrust of the action was that Microsoft was using its monopolistic power to shut out the competition, which in turn did not benefit the American public:

> To the detriment of consumers, however, Microsoft has done much more than develop innovative browsing software of commendable quality and offer it bundled with Windows at no additional charge. As has been shown, Microsoft also engaged in a concerted series of actions designed to protect the applications barrier to entry, and hence its monopoly power, from a variety of middleware threats, including Netscape's Web browser and Sun's implementation of Java. Many of these actions have harmed consumers in ways that are immediate and easily discernible. They have also caused less direct, but nevertheless serious and far-reaching, consumer harm by distorting competition.
>
> (Department of Justice 1999: 204)

Gates himself appeared on the witness stand; his deposition videotaped for subsequent scrutiny. The press noted that Gates at times appeared to have little respect for the proceedings, being highly evasive, even obstructive in his answers, constantly challenging the opposition legal team to define terms and explain principles. In a *BusinessWeek* article on 19 November 1998, journalist Ellen Neuborne observed:

> By most measures, the flesh-and-blood Gates has come off far less admirably in his videotaped performance at his company's antitrust trial. He squirms and hedges. He argues with prosecutors over the definition of commonly used words, including 'we' and 'compete.' Early rounds of his deposition show him offering obfuscatory answers and saying 'I don't recall' so many times that even the presiding judge had to chuckle. Worse, many of the technology chief's denials and pleas of ignorance have been directly refuted by prosecutors with snippets of E-mail Gates both sent and received. (Neuborne 1999)

Yet despite this 'unflattering portrait caught on tape' and the fact that the prosecutors were trying to portray Gates as an 'overgrown schoolyard bully' (Ibid.), Neuborne noted that Gates' public popularity was relatively unchanged by the case. She cited a *BusinessWeek*/Harris poll in which 32 per cent of those surveyed said that they actually admired Gates (dropping a little from 37 per cent the previous June), but those who actually disliked him remained constant at just 8 per cent.

The case reached one of its several summits on 5 November 1999, when Judge Jackson issued his findings of fact. He held that Microsoft had committed multiple acts of monopolization or attempted monopolization and violations of the 1890 Sherman Antitrust Act. On 7 June the following year came the real bombshell. The court ordered that Microsoft be broken up into different companies, particularly between its operating system and software development divisions.

Gates was not going to go meekly with this decision, and Microsoft immediately appealed the judgement to the District of Columbia Circuit Court of Appeals. Gates released an impassioned statement to the general press, furiously highlighting what he saw as government attempts to control a very American success story:

> This is clearly the most massive attempt at government regulation of the technology industry ever, and it was conceived by the government and imposed by this ruling without a single day of testimony or scrutiny. This plan would undermine our high-tech economy, hurt consumers, make computers harder to use, and impact thousands of other companies and employees throughout the high-tech industry. Microsoft feels we have a very strong case on appeal. It's important we stay focused on building great software and that people understand that this kind of regulation would really hurt the high-tech economy.

Gates clearly saw the case as having negative implications for wider US innovation. Yet on 28 June 2001, the DC Circuit Court judge overturned the judgement against Microsoft, on the basis that Judge Jackson had violated the US Code of Conduct for judges by speaking to the press about the case. The DOJ's investigation findings of fact remained in place, however. So, to avoid further antitrust actions, Microsoft and the DOJ reached an agreement that Microsoft, among other measures, had to share its application programming interfaces with third-party companies, plus a three-panel 'Technical Committee' would have access to Microsoft's systems, processes, documents and source code to monitor compliance. The agreement obligations would expire in 2007.

NEW ERA

Much had changed personally for Bill Gates by the time the DOJ court case was wrapped up. He was getting older – he turned 40 years old in 1995 and although still youthful for his age the wispy and unkempt young man who had driven the business in the early years was now a thing of the past. He was also now a husband – in

Bill and Melinda Gates, seen here shortly after their marriage on New Year's Day in January 1994. Together they founded one of the greatest philanthropic organisations in modern history.

1994, he married Melinda French, a Microsoft product manager, in the process finding a partnership that to a large extent would define the direction of his life over the next three decades. (More about both Gates' marriage and his life beyond Microsoft will be covered in subsequent chapters.) The first two of his three children had also arrived: Jennifer in April 1996 and Rory in May 1999, later joined by Phoebe in September 2002. In the past, the young Bill Gates had frequently clashed with employees who had family commitments outside an expected round-the-clock duty to Microsoft. Now Gates was a family man himself.

Then on 13 January 2000 came a shock change in the Microsoft leadership. Gates announced that he was stepping down as the company's CEO, handing over the day-to-day running of the company to Steve Ballmer, who was also company president by this time. Gates would instead take the title of chief software architect. He explained that this new role 'will allow me to spend almost 100% of my time on new software technologies. It's an exciting evolution for me and a very good transition for the company. Although I've been able to spend more time on our technical strategy since naming Steve as president in July 1998, I felt that the opportunities for Microsoft were incredible, yet our structure wasn't optimal to really take advantage of them to the degree that we should.' (Quoted in *Forbes*, 2000).

Naturally, the press scrutinized his decision suspiciously. Was it taken to relieve some pressure on the company during the ongoing DOJ case, especially since to a large extent the person of Bill Gates and the company of Microsoft were regarded as coterminous entities? Or was it just to do exactly what Gates said, get to grips with a new era of technology that was going to be profoundly different from previous decades? Another question was asked – how would Gates now work with Ballmer, whose management style and visions of the future didn't always align with those of his former boss? Would Gates remain the power behind the throne?

Even with the 2000 decision, Gates was still integral to Microsoft and its future. But it seemed to set in train Gates' gradual practical disengagement from Microsoft. Jumping forward eight years, on 15 June 2008, Microsoft released the following announcement:

Microsoft Corp. today announced that effective July 2008 Bill Gates, chairman, will transition out of a day-to-day role in the company to spend more time on his global health and education work at the Bill & Melinda Gates Foundation. The company

By the 2000s, Bill Gates was recognised not only as a triumphant entrepreneur, but also as one of the planet's most powerful individuals via his influence over global computing and development aid. Here he shares a stage with President Bill Clinton at the Time Magazine Global Health Summit in New York, November 2005.

announced a two-year transition process to ensure that there is a smooth and orderly transfer of Gates' daily responsibilities, and said that after July 2008 Gates would continue to serve as the company's chairman and an advisor on key development projects. (Microsoft 2006)

It is clear, therefore, that Gates saw his relationship with Microsoft change fundamentally in the first decade of the 2000s, although it would be a particularly long goodbye – Gates only resigned from the Microsoft board in 2020. As subsequent chapters will show, Gates was far from slipping into retirement; life outside Microsoft would almost be as dynamic as life inside it. Here we will maintain our focus on the years 2000–08. Many accounts of this period at Microsoft reflect on the emerging tension between Ballmer and Gates, as the two men wrestled over their visions of the company in the new millennium.

TRIUMPH AND DISASTER

The 2000s saw Microsoft's core business – the Windows operating systems and applications software – still dominating the market on the PC. Windows 95 evolved into Windows 98, then to Windows 2000 and, in 2001, Windows XP, a fresh interface based on the NT architecture. Generally, each of these iterations of Windows brought approval from reviewers and buyers, and strong sales figures. Then Windows Vista launched in 2007 at the end of a long and fairly troubled development period. Vista introduced a host of new features and improvements, but market reception was less enthusiastic this time, noting problems over its functionality, intrusive authorization controls, licence restrictions and high performance demands. Retail sales of Vista ceased in October 2010, Vista being succeeded by Windows 7. But even given the slightly erratic evolutionary progress of Windows, it was still the software on the majority of people's computers. MS Office, meanwhile, was *the* primary office software for both PC and Apple users.

Although, as explained above, Gates' titular relationship to Microsoft was changing, he was still very much the face of Microsoft. Gates was still front of house for the launch of Vista. On 30 January 2007, he led a launch presentation for Vista and for the new version of MS Office at the British Library in London, UK. Gates gave a long, emboldened speed about how he saw Vista plugging into core trends in networked computing, with digital interconnectivity linking different spheres of human activity like a spider diagram of progress:

> Now, in Windows Vista, we have the foundation to take things to a whole new level. So instead of just saying that it's about the Internet, now we talk about how it's about the digital workstyle and the digital lifestyle. And the number of things that will be revolutionized on top of the Windows Vista platform is quite large. The way that people buy and sell products. The way we think of telephony – the end of the so-called dedicated PBX. The revolution of television, where you're not limited to broadcast channels and just the popular items. And where even the shows themselves now will be personalized, where the news items that you care about will be longer. If it's an educational show, you'll have the opportunity to interact. Even the advertising will be targeted as well. We'll be taking entertainment to a whole new level, where you can find the music that you're interested in, or

play games that are a whole new level of realism, and connecting up to other people around the world. It's fair to say that even education, we believe, will be changed very dramatically. We've done special versions of Windows, like Media Center, which is about this TV and entertainment change. And the Tablet version, which is about letting people go to meetings and take their notes. But perhaps most interestingly, letting students have a device that allows them to work without paper textbooks, and yet interact and share in richer ways. So we're just at the very beginning of that. We've just begun to see what we can do.
(Microsoft 2007)

Looking back from the present, some elements of this speech appear either naive or unsettling. For example, targeted advertising is now

Bill Gates talks with reporters and customers about the launch of Windows 98 in June 1998. In total, this version of Windows sold approximately 58 million licences before being superseded by products such as Windows XP in the early 2000s.

a source of government-level concern about privacy, not progress to be embraced. But back then, Gates was selling little short of a revolution of self, each human integrated into a greater whole via digital means, being empowered in the process.

The speech, although focused on Vista, evidently sees Microsoft's future going in many more directions than just Windows and the GUI. Gates had long recognized that the internet would transform hardware, platforms and lifestyles, the new commercial targets popping up thick and fast and requiring a fast hand to shoot them first. The problem was, for both Microsoft and Gates, that by the early 2000s, in many areas, Microsoft was already proving slow on the draw.

Apple, for example, had come roaring back, having survived (just) a perilous period during the 1990s. But from the late 1990s, the company was back under the fiery, brilliant leadership of Steve Jobs, and times were a-changing. In May 1998, Apple launched the iMac computer. Its see-through, teardrop-shaped coloured shell was like nothing else seen on a desk. Here was computer *cool*. The iMac was sexy, modern and trend-setting, but under the hood it was also innovative, with features such as USB ports and pre-installed internet connectivity (there was no external modem). It flew off the shelves, selling 800,000 units in the first five months of release. Similarly catching was the iBook, the first in the line of highly desirable Apple laptops, launched in April 1999. It would mature through its teenage years into the MacBook Pro, launched in 2007, powered by Intel processors. Beyond the hardware, the Apple GUI and software was also leaping ahead. Apple computers came with a raft of family-branded programs, including iMovie, iTunes, iPhoto and iLife. In 2001, Apple also unveiled a new Unix operating system, Mac OS X. It was beautiful, simple, graceful to use, without the 'clutter' many felt had now accrued in Windows systems.

Apple also led the way in portable devices. The public was enthralled by the iPod portable digital music player, unveiled in October 2001. More than 100 million units were sold over the next six years, aided by the introduction of the iTunes Store in 2003, giving an unprecedented easy download of millions of tunes. (The service recorded more than 5 billion downloads in five years.)

Apple's strengths hardened around stunning branding, robust build quality, clean lines of functionality and an oozing sense of coolness. The company also straddled both hardware and software, bringing the two together with seamless harmony. Windows-running PCs were still by far the best-sellers, not least because they were so much cheaper than the high-end Macs, but Apple was certainly taking bigger chunks of the computing real estate.

Apple was not the only one forging ahead. The 2000s was the era in which the video gaming consoles – entertainment-dedicated machines with high-end graphics and electrifying gameplay – went into global overdrive. Back in 1994–95, Sony Interactive Entertainment had set the pace with the release of its now-iconic PlayStation, followed by the release of the updated Playstation one [sic] and the (literally and metaphorically) game-changing PlayStation 2 in 2000. The sales of these machines and their games were out-the-ballpark impressive; by December 2003 alone, more than 102 million PlayStation and Playstation one consoles had been shipped; the PlayStation 2 shipped more than 100 million consoles in its first five years. Nor was Sony the only player in this game. The big-league competitors were the Sega Saturn, the Nintendo 64 (which sold 300,000 units on its first day) and the Nintendo GameCube.

So where were Gates and Microsoft in this race? Both Gates and Ballmer were well aware that they were falling behind. For more than two decades, Microsoft's horizons had been defined by PCs, operating systems, software applications, languages. Games consoles were something truly new. There had been some efforts at collaboration between Microsoft and the big gaming companies. For example, on 7 April 1998, Microsoft and Sony issued a joint press release, which included a co-operative note from Gates:

(Redmond, WA and New York, NY) April 7, 1998 – Microsoft Corporation and Sony Corporation today announced plans to begin collaboration to create a convergence of the personal computer and consumer AV electronics platforms.

To facilitate the fusion of the PC and AV platforms, the two companies plan to cross-license key software technologies. Sony intends to license Microsoft's Windows CE operating system [a version of Windows designed for small computers] for use in certain future products. Similarly, Microsoft intends to license Sony's Home Networking Module for use with certain versions of Windows CE. [...]

'Sony's ability to develop consumer electronics products with broad consumer appeal is second to none,' said Bill Gates, CEO of Microsoft Corporation. 'We hope that our combined efforts will give birth to even more exciting products and applications in both the computer and AV entertainment arenas.'
(Microsoft/Sony 1998)

But beyond the apparent spirit of shared opportunity, the press also alleged that the relationship between Gates and Sony was at times less than cordial. One story is that Gates had a meeting with Sony CEO Nobuyuki Idei prior to the release of the PlayStation 2 to discuss whether Sony might use Microsoft programming tools, but Gates was turned away empty-handed, allegedly making him furious. Idei later told Ken Auletta of the *New Yorker*: 'With Microsoft, open architecture means Microsoft architecture.' (Scoglio 2018).

Microsoft would ultimately enter the games console market independently. In 1999, Gates personally oversaw hiring a team of sharp engineers to create Microsoft's first console, running what became known as a 'beauty contest' to recruit the best and the brightest in the field, capable of designing a product that would explode on to the market. That product was the Xbox. It was unveiled with great fanfare on 3 January 2001 in Las Vegas, Gates taking to the stage alongside wrestler Dwayne 'The Rock' Johnson.

Thus began what became known as the 'console wars'. Xbox, given extra juice via popular games such as *Halo* and *Dead or Alive*, hit the ground running and by 2005 had sold 24 million units. Although those figures are impressive, by that time the PlayStation 2 had sold 100 million units, with Sony still the market leader; Microsoft had taken the lead over Nintendo, however.

The console wars would stay hot and bloody throughout the 2000s. Microsoft upped its game with more powerful versions of the Xbox, especially the Xbox 360 on 12 May 2005, although the rush to get that to market resulted in some serious hardware problems making their way into the release product, issues that would eventually cost Microsoft more than $1 billion to resolve. Nevertheless, Xbox 360 went on to sell 85.8 million units by July 2022, equal to that of the PlayStation 3. The Xbox Kinect was released in 2010, featuring state-of-the-art motion-activated gameplay, although this system didn't gain enough traction and was discontinued by 2017.

The intensity of the console wars was later reflected in a 2013 episode of the taboo-breaking animated series *South Park*. The episode, irreverently entitled 'Titties and Dragons', featured a jacked-up muscular Gates and Sony CEO Kazuo 'Kaz' Hirai fighting to the death in front of the wayward South Park boys – Gates wins with a brutal kill move worthy of any fight game.

But outside games consoles, there were other battlegrounds. In 2000, for example, Google became the world's leading search

Bill Gates first attended the World Economic Forum (WEF) in 1998. Ever since, he has been a prominent figure of this annual gathering of the world's most influential leaders at Davos, Switzerland, Here he speaks with U2 frontman Bono and British Prime Minister Tony Blair at the WEF meeting in January 2005.

engine. Given that this position was attained just two years after Google was founded, this achievement must have been particularly galling to Gates. Microsoft released a new version of its MSN search engine in 2005, but by this time Google was sprinting way ahead and would open a distance Microsoft could not close. But search was just one aspect in which Microsoft would be overtaken.

THE SMARTPHONE QUESTION

By the end of the 1990s, there were the first inklings that the future of computing might lie in smartphones, handheld devices that combined both telephony and advanced computing. The precursor to the smartphone was the personal digital assistant (PDA), essentially a handheld computer with reduced functionality compared to their desktop or laptop relatives. Microsoft had already entered the market for PDA operating systems with Windows CE. But smartphone technology began to gather exponential innovation, cost reductions and capabilities from the late 1990s, spreading out from Japan to the rest of the world. Hardware became the exciting terrain of this advance. Research In Motion (RIM)'s Blackberry smartphone, for example, was the must-have business tool of the 90s, but numerous other companies began pumping out phones to the masses, including Nokia, Ericsson, Sony, Qualcomm, Motorola and Kyocera. The new generation of smartphones now featured video and still cameras, full-colour LCD screens and cellular internet access.

Microsoft sought to stay in the race through its Windows Mobile operating system (released in April 2000 as a development of Windows CE), which primarily competed for market share with Symbian and Palm OS. But here lay the roots of a future problem.

When we look at interviews given by Gates and Ballmer in the mid-2000s, the Microsoft outlook still seems very software-oriented. Gates was interviewed by Peter Rojas for *Endgadget* in May 2005. Rojas interrogated Gates closely on Microsoft's plans for taking Windows Mobile forward and also asked whether Gates' goal was to have the same impact with Windows Mobile in the smartphone market as MS Windows had had in the PC market: 'Well there'll always be tons of operating systems. There'll always be tons of software stacks in mobile phones. We're trying to make the best software we can and we have no shortage of ideas where we can make that phone way better than it is today.' (Rojas 2005).

Gates here sees the smartphone market as a software arena. But in 2007, the arena was reconfigured by two events. The first was that Apple launched its iPhone, a complete revisioning of the smartphone concept that instantly rendered great swathes of the smartphone market either looking dated at best or obsolete at worst. In 2007, Apple sold 1.4 million iPhones; in the following year, that number leapt to 11.63 million and in 2010 it sold just shy of 40 million units, producing revenues of $25 billion.

For Microsoft, the shock of the iPhone was profound, but 2007 was to bring a compounding blow. In November that year, the Open Handset Alliance (OHA), a consortium of 34 major tech companies led by Google, announced the Android mobile phone operating system. (The OHA would over time grow to incorporate 84 companies.) Contra Microsoft's way of operating, Android was open source, which opened the floodgates for adoption. The first Android phone (the HTC Dream) was launched in 2008, but Android quickly came to hold 80 per cent of the smartphone operating system market.

The Microsoft suite of software has, collectively, had a profound effect on shaping global education. Bill Gates has described education as 'the most powerful tool you can use to change the world'. Here he answers questions from Chinese students while demonstrating a Microsoft tablet PC during a visit to a middle school in Beijing on 1 July 2004.

Bill Gates has received numerous academic honours. Here he is presented with an honourary doctorate from China's Tsinghua University in April 2007.

The combined thrusts of Apple and Android squeezed Microsoft's authority in the emerging smartphone era, in both hardware and software. Too late, Gates sought to get into the hardware game, although how willingly he took this step is questionable (see below). In 2014, Microsoft purchased Nokia's Devices and Service Division for $7.2 billion, Microsoft forming a Microsoft Mobile subsidiary to sell Nokia devices.

This decision, fronted by Steve Ballmer, turned out to be one of the biggest strategic failures in Microsoft's history. In the following year, the company took a $7.6 billion write-down and was compelled to shed 7,800 jobs, mainly in its phone business. In 2016, Microsoft sold its loss-making cell phone business and in 2017 also announced it was no longer developing new Windows phones.

Microsoft was comprehensively beaten in the smartphone race. The public evaluation of why this occurred has included an assessment of relations between Gates and Ballmer, which reportedly changed significantly after the former ostensibly handed over the reins to the latter. Certainly, Gates has deep personal regrets about his part in the smartphone debacle. During an interview at the World Economic Forum in Davos, Switzerland on 22 January 2016, he said that allowing Google to develop Android (Google purchased the original Android Inc. company in 2005) was his 'greatest mistake ever', one connected with his person 'mismanagement' plus the distractions of various antitrust cases (Scipioni 2019). (Microsoft faced another major antitrust legal action within the European Union from 2004, which eventually resulted in the company being fined €497 million [US$613 million], ordered to divulge certain protocols to competitors, and to produce a new version of its Windows XP platform.) Gates wistfully acknowledged that if Microsoft had grabbed the smartphone market. 'We would be *the* company. But oh well.' (Ibid.).

Steve Ballmer has also shared his take on events from around this period. We should remember that by the time Ballmer took over as CEO from Gates, the two men were exceptionally close friends – Ballmer was even Gates' best man at Gates' wedding to Melinda. But much seemed to have changed once Ballmer took over. In an interview with *Vanity Fair*, published in November 2016, Ballmer stated that in the first year of being CEO: 'We had a very miserable year. Bill didn't know how to work for anybody, and I didn't know how to manage Bill. I'm not sure I ever learned the latter.' *The Wall Street Journal* had earlier reported problems with the transition, reporting shouting matches and confrontations between the two men, with Ballmer allegedly saying that once Gates had left, 'I'm not going to need him for anything. That's the principle. Use him, yes, need him, no.' (Guth 2008).

In an interview for Bloomberg TV in 2016, Ballmer saw the smartphone issue as the catalyst for much of the breakdown in relations: 'I think there was a fundamental disagreement about how important it was to be in the hardware business. [...] Things came to a climax around what to do with the phone business. I certainly wanted to buy Nokia, but the board at first disagreed with that, then came back and said that the company should go ahead even though I had decided to leave. [...] If executed in a certain way I think it made a lot of sense.' (Ballmer 2016). Ballmer argued that Microsoft should have entered the smartphone market much sooner but was tripped by the distraction of the Vista release, which had taken up large volumes of engineer time.

It is hard to define the full impact, or indeed full extent, of Gates' struggle with Ballmer during this period. Certainly, it seems that Gates was less comfortable in navigating the landscape of the 2000s, as the world shifted its focus away from PCs to other devices. Gates was, after all, *the* PC pioneer. Also, by the 2000s, Microsoft was a vast company, possibly losing some of the intellectual and corporate agility of those early improvisational years.

But we must not let Microsoft's failure in some battles lead us to the conclusion that it had lost the war. Microsoft in the first decade of the 2000s was still one of the most powerful forces in global computing. Bill Gates' original vision of a computer on every desk in every home, running Microsoft software, had not come literally true, but the interface between much of humanity and the digital world was still designed and built by Microsoft.

Gates would remain heavily involved with Microsoft after 2008. In February 2014, he stepped down from his position as chairman of the company but retained a role as a 'technical advisor' to Satya Nadella, who took over as Microsoft CEO in 2013 after Ballmer left the company for fresh fields. Gates clarified his working life division to the press: 'I'm thrilled that Satya has asked me to step up, substantially increasing the time that I spend at the company. I'll have over a third of my time available to meet with product groups, and it'll be fun to define this next round of products working together.' (Quoted in Kastrenakes 2014).

COMING OF AGE

In 2015, Microsoft celebrated its 40th birthday. In response, it was entirely fitting that Bill Gates compose a letter to mark the occasion. The contents of the letter are classic to his style and were run in the world's press. Regardless of what had gone before, Gates is not a man to live in the past, and following the mild nostalgia of the first paragraphs he quickly turns to future-forward optimism:

Tomorrow is a special day: Microsoft's 40th anniversary.

Early on, Paul Allen and I set the goal of a computer on every desk and in every home. It was a bold idea and a lot of people thought we were out of our minds to imagine it was possible. It is amazing to think about how far computing has come since

The end of a digital era arrived on 15 June 2006 – Bill Gates, as Chairman of Microsoft, announced that he was transitioning out of the day-to-day role in the company he founded more than 40 years previously. He here makes that announcement alongside Microsoft CEO Steve Ballmer (left). Gates stated that his focus would be more on the activities of the Bill and Melinda Gates Foundation. Gates told journalists that 'Steve is the best CEO for Microsoft I could imagine.'

then, and we can all be proud of the role Microsoft played in that revolution.

Today though, I am thinking much more about Microsoft's future than its past. I believe computing will evolve faster in the next 10 years than it ever has before. We already live in a multi-platform world, and computing will become even more pervasive. We are nearing the point where computers and robots will be able to see, move, and interact naturally, unlocking many new applications and empowering people even more.

[...]

In the coming years, Microsoft has the opportunity to reach even more people and organizations around the world. Technology is still out of reach for many people, because it is complex or expensive, or they simply do not have access. So I hope you will think about what you can do to make the power of technology accessible to everyone, to connect people to each other, and make personal computing available everywhere even as the very notion of what a PC delivers makes its way into all devices.

We have accomplished a lot together during our first 40 years and empowered countless businesses and people to realize their full potential. But what matters most now is what we do next. Thank you for helping make Microsoft a fantastic company now and for decades to come.

Gates would finally step down from the Microsoft board in 2020 to focus squarely upon his philanthropic and charitable work. But as time moves on, it is clear that part of Microsoft will forever belong to Bill Gates.

CHAPTER 5
GIVING BACK

In January 2008, Bill Gates was on the cusp of a great change in his life's direction. He was looking at stepping away from his day-to-day role in Microsoft, letting others take the helm of the company he had diligently steered since the 1970s. But what wouldn't change was his scale of ambition. He still wanted to change the world, just now in different ways.

Gates gave a speech at the World Economic Forum in Davos that January in which he took an uncharacteristically self-reflective tone (lightened by some humour) before throwing down a challenge both to himself and the influential audience:

As you all may know, in July I'll make a big career change. I'm not worried; I believe I'm still marketable. I'm a self-starter, I'm proficient in Microsoft Office. I guess that's it. Also I'm learning how to give money away. So, this is the last time I'll attend Davos as a full-time employee of Microsoft. Some of us are lucky enough to arrive at moments in life when we can pause, reflect on our work, and say: 'This is great. It's fun, exciting, and useful; I could do this forever.' But the passing of time forces each of us to take stock and ask: What have I accomplished so far? What do I still want to accomplish? Thirty years ago, 20 years ago, 10 years ago, my focus was totally on how the magic of software could change the world. I saw that breakthroughs in technology could solve key problems. And they do, increasingly, for billions of people. But breakthroughs change lives primarily where people can afford to buy them, only where there is economic demand, and economic demand is not the same as economic need. There are billions of people who need the great inventions of the computer age, and many more basic needs as well, but they have no way of expressing their needs in ways that matter to the market, so they go without. If we are going to have a chance of changing their lives, we need another level of innovation. Not just technology innovation, we need system innovation, and that's what I want to discuss with you here in Davos today.

(World Economic Forum 2008)

This was radical stuff. Gates was explaining a fundamental reappraisal of his life's direction, refocusing on the needs of the world's poor and disadvantaged, rather than the privileged masses of the developed world. But many of the challenges ahead would remain at heart technological, an arena in which Gates excels.

GIVING PLEDGE

In June 2010, Bill Gates, Melinda Gates and their close friend Warren Buffett (also one of the richest individuals in the world) announced the launch of the 'Giving Pledge'. It expressed a bold model for future philanthropy. The signatories to the pledge committed themselves to giving away the majority of their wealth to good causes over the course of their lifetimes. In the original pledge letter, Bill and Melinda laid out the groundwork for their decision:

Both of us were fortunate to grow up with parents who taught us some tremendously important values. Work hard. Show respect. Have a sense of humor. And if life happens to bless you with talent or treasure, you have a responsibility to use those gifts as well and as wisely as you possibly can. Now we hope to pass this example on to our own children.

We feel very lucky to have the chance to work together in giving back the resources we are stewards of. By joining the Giving Pledge effort, we're certain our giving will be more effective because of the time we will spend with this group. We look forward to sharing what a wonderful experience this has been for us and learning from the experience of others.

(Bill and Melinda Gates 2010)

The letter expresses gratitude and indebtedness, a desire to give back to the world that had already given them so much. The wider body of the pledge outlined two main areas they would target in their efforts: education for the disadvantaged and challenges in global health, especially the eradication of preventable diseases. These were ambitious objectives, normally tackled at governmental level. Yet many others soon signed up to the Giving Pledge. By August 2010, there were 40 signatories with an aggregated wealth of $125 billion. As of December 2022, the number of signatories had grown to 236 individuals from 28 countries.

Bill Gates has kept his faith with the Giving Pledge. Since its establishment, he has poured prodigious volumes of personal wealth into the transformational causes of the Bill & Melinda Gates Foundation (BMGF), plus a wide variety of other charitable projects. Based on calculations made from public statements, some estimate that Bill Gates intends to give away more than 99 per cent of his wealth by the end of his life (Mohr 2021).

But the scale of Gates' philanthropic work is not just limited by his personal finances. The BMGF has become the second largest charitable foundation in the world, with financial power that rivals or even exceeds that of many small nation states. At the time of writing, it has 1,736 employees in offices dotted strategically around the globe. By the end of 2021, the total value of its grant payments since inception had reached an astonishing $65.6 billion, the total of the endowment peaking at about $70 billion. From inception through to 2022, Bill and Melinda had given the foundation $59.1 billion of their own money (Warren Buffett added another $35.7 billion). As we shall see, these figures have had a genuine global impact on the ground.

For those more accustomed to the characterization of Gates as an arch capitalist, his work in the charitable and not-for-profit sectors can generate some cognitive dissonance. Certainly, at Microsoft, Gates forged his reputation as a hard driver of profit, known for his merciless manoeuvring against rivals. Steve Jobs once told *Rolling Stone* reporter Jeff Goodell that 'The trouble with Bill is that he wants to take a nickel for himself out of every dollar that passes through his hands.' (Goodell 2014). Gates remains a shrewd operator when it comes to finances and investment, and he is still philosophically wedded to the profit motive in business, especially when it acts as an incentive for innovation where otherwise there would be none.

But Gates has also come to revision profit as possibility, the possibility of reforming and reshaping the world to make it a better place for its inhabitants. His efforts through the BMGF are not without controversies. Gates' current reputation in the press and social media oscillates somewhere between techno super-villain plotting global takeover and reforming saint fighting for the poor and disadvantaged. Neither extreme is accurate. Rather, Gates appears driven by genuine altruism, but also by rational optimism in which the world is viewed as an imperfect system that needs to be fixed through the application of innovation, technology and scientific progress. In some ways, therefore, Gates' charitable work represents a continuation of Microsoft, but in very different domains.

STARTING UP

Philanthropy had always been part of the Gates family's lifeblood. Both of his parents had been exemplary activists, fundraisers and givers for social important causes, operating from the sense that wealth obligated spending on far more than just self-indulgence and lavish lifestyles. Gates' personal engagement with social activism actually began during the heyday of Microsoft's success in the 1990s. In 1994, Bill and Melinda established the William H. Gates Foundation, the organization taking the name of Bill's father, who would act as the foundation manager with an endowment of $106 million (Reference for Business 2023). The foundation cast a broad benevolent net, raising money for global health problems but also for issues closer to home in the American north-west.

Bill Gates' strategy for effecting social change added another stratum in 1997, when Bill and Melinda established the Gates Library Foundation, which tied together Bill's unifying vision of education and technology. At this time in North American history, less than a quarter of public libraries had internet access and in many cases that access was only for staff, not for patrons. Gates wanted to drive computers and the internet into US and Canadian libraries in low-income areas, to iron out some of the knowledge imbalances between rich and poor. Microsoft already had some experience in this area. In December 1995, Microsoft had launched the Libraries Online initiative, which had the similar goal of taking information technology into isolated or poorly funded public libraries. The pilot programme saw 200 libraries across North America receive a total of $17 million of funding for software.

The press release that accompanied the launch of the Libraries Foundation included Gates' personal testimony about the

The Gates Library Foundation had a measurable impact upon hundreds of schools and communities across the United States. Here Gates, with LA Mayor Richard Riordan at his side, provides guidance to students at a public library in Los Angeles on 27 November 1996, the same day he announced a $1.1 million donation to the city's libraries.

significance of libraries in his own life and the educational impact offered by digital access:

> Since I was a kid, libraries have played an important role in my life. In the past couple of years I have had the opportunity to visit many libraries and see first hand how people are using personal computers and the Internet to do anything from look for a job to research a term paper. Witnessing the empowerment this technology has given people underscores my belief that computers can really make a difference in the lives of others.
> (BMGF)

The argument for spreading digital access has a democratizing impetus. Gates sees those who are shut out of the digital future as deprived persons, regardless of what other assets they have on hand. When Gates addressed the 123rd commencement at Stanford University in 2014, he saw this digital democratization as informing Microsoft from the very start:

> When Paul Allen and I started Microsoft, we wanted to bring the power of computers and software to the people – and that was the kind of rhetoric we used. One of the pioneering books in the field had a raised fist on the cover, and it was called *Computer Lib*. At that time, only big businesses could buy computers. We wanted to offer the same power to regular people and democratize computing. By the 1990s, we saw how profoundly personal computers could empower people. But that success created a new dilemma: If rich kids got computers and poor kids didn't, then technology would make inequality worse. That ran counter to our core belief:

> Technology should benefit everybody. So we worked to close the digital divide. I made it a priority at Microsoft, and Melinda and I made it an early priority at our foundation, donating personal computers to public libraries to make sure everyone had access. (Stanford 2014)

In 1999, the Gates Library Foundation was renamed Gates Learning Foundation, reflecting a broader range of educational interests and investment. This foundation included the Millennium Scholars Program, which over the next two decades would put 20,000 minority students through college on scholarships.

According to the BMGF website, a pivotal moment in Bill and Melinda's altruistic outreach came in 1997 when, triggered by an investigative news article, they read the 1993 World Development Report. It was sobering reading. The report illustrated the devastating human attrition inflicted globally by preventable diseases, especially upon the young and the hungry. Inspired to act, Gates wrote a letter to his father saying, 'Dad, maybe we can do something about this.'

Another moment of insight came in the mid-1990s when Gates made a trip to impoverished ghetto areas of South Africa. One particular township had just a single electrical outlet, leading Gates to conclude (in interview for *The New York Times Magazine*): 'I looked around and thought, Hmmm, computers may not be the highest priority in this particular place.'

Gates was kindling what would flare into an abiding passion for work in the developing world, particularly in the field of healthcare. Much of these parts of our planet, and especially Africa, have been neglected by Western innovations in medicine because they do not provide the market affluence for high returns on sales and investment. Determined to reverse this trend, Gates turned his efforts towards key initiatives. Noting, for example, that malaria killed more than 1 million people worldwide every year, in 1999 the Gates Foundation put $50 million into establishing a Malaria Vaccine Initiative – bear in mind that global spending on malaria research at this time only totalled about $60 million. The foundation also funded a Children's Vaccine Program to the tune of $100 million, targeting diseases such as diphtheria, measles, polio, tetanus and whooping cough. Further large sums of money were diverted into research into vaccines for Acquired Immunodeficiency Syndrome (AIDS), a particularly cruel disease that was having a disproportionately destructive effect in sub-Saharan Africa. Other health objectives included funding for the detection and cure of cervical cancer.

Bill Gates (centre) with Arunma Oteh (left) and Dr Francoise Ndayishmiye at the 2009 London launch of the DATA Report, which monitors promises made by the G8 in 2005 to fight extreme poverty in Africa. to Africa.

By the year 2000, the Gates Foundation was spending an estimated $400 million every year on global health initiatives. In the same year, the foundation pledged $750 million in a five-year support programme to the newly formed Gavi: The Vaccine Alliance organization, which was committed to large-scale vaccination programmes in the developing world. The foundation also publicly committed itself to supporting the delivery of the United Nations' Millennium Development Goals by 2015. Balancing out their global reach with problems much closer to home, in 2000, Bill and Melinda also launched Sound Families, a project to tackle family homelessness in the Puget Sound region of Washington State.

GLOBAL IMPACT

As Bill and Melinda Gates' humanitarian activities grew to greater international significance, it was time for a rationalization. In 2000, they consolidated their activities into the Bill & Melinda Gates Foundation (BMGF). The impact of this single organization on the well-being of the planet is profound in scale and genuinely life-changing for millions of people across the globe. On 13 July 2022, Bill Gates posted a rather laconic tweet. Reading between the lines, we start to perceive the vaulted ambition of the Foundation: 'I am very proud of the foundation's role in helping solve big problems like preventing pandemics, reducing childhood deaths, eradicating diseases, improving food security and climate adaptation, achieving gender equality, and improving educational outcomes.' (Twitter 2022)

The BMGF is clearly not a single-issue institution. The organization is structured according to operational divisions according to focus. Here I will provide an overview of each, not merely to highlight the landmark work undertaken but also to reveal more about Gates' beliefs and priorities. Not only does the work of the BMGF express Gates' belief in the fusion of science and altruism, but it also reminds us of Gates' advocacy of what he calls the 'digital nervous system' (DNS) – in many fields of human endeavour, we can't accomplish anything meaningful without information. (The DNS is explained more fully in the next chapter.)

We start with the Foundation's Gender Equality Division, which is described as follows: 'Our Gender Equality Division works to ensure women and girls in Africa and South Asia can enjoy good health, make their own choices, earn their own money, and be leaders in their societies.' (BMGF 2023). Its areas of effort include: social reforms to enhance the positions of women and adolescent girls; family planning, ensuring that women in the developing world have access to effective birth control; maternal, newborn and child health; advancing women's leadership roles, 'particularly in the fields of health, law and economics'; and providing financial support so women can generate their own incomes. Although we must never forget Melinda's equal and driving role within the Foundation, we can argue that this division of the BMGF at least partly reflects the very strong female role models throughout Gates' life (especially his mother and his wife), plus a serious attitude about the logic behind women's issues. Indeed, the Foundation website states that: 'We believe that the undervaluing of women and girls is at the root of every problem our foundation is working to solve.'

Gates is a clear advocate of equality. But at the same time he looks at the issue from a specific ideological and pragmatic stand-point. In November 2020, Gates did two podcasts with the US

President Barack Obama presents the Presidential Medal of Freedom to Bill and Melinda Gates during a ceremony in the East Room of the White House on 22 November, 2016 in Washington, DC

actress Rashida Jones. In the second of these, the pair went deep into the weeds of gender and wealth inequality. The latter, however, raises potentially awkward questions about the disparities of rich and poor. Jones asked him if equality was 'inevitable', to which Gates gave a politically nuanced reply:

> The system that tries to equalize all outcomes is communism. That system, in terms of incentives and freedom of choice and rewarding hard work and innovation has worked very poorly. Some of the most miserable lives, shortest lives, in the world are where we have that ideology still in place. That's failed. How you combine a desire to have some mobility, safety net, and yet encourage hard

work and innovation, [that] every country's still struggling to find that balance.
(Gates/Jones 2020)

Throughout the interview, Gates pushes back against Jones' efforts to suggest more left-leaning political solutions to inequality. Gates has been strongly opposed to top-down political compulsions of equality, part of his abiding dislike for communist and socialist political solutions. Rather, he seeks to achieve equalities through opening doors of opportunity, removing practical, educational and health barriers to allow individual strengths to flourish and success to follow naturally. He is at heart an individualist, who also cares about what happens at the societal level.

The Global Development Division of BMGF 'focuses on improving the delivery of high-impact health products and services to the world's poorest communities and helps countries expand access to health coverage.' (BMGF 2023). One of its foci is disaster relief work, but the biggest-hitting programmes within the foundation are related to immunization. For Gates, there is an inescapable logic to a vaccination programme. For a few dollars per shot, you protect a person against common diseases that kill unvaccinated people in their hundreds of thousands. A well-vaccinated country, therefore, is protecting its well-being, population, economy and general future.

BMGF immunization programmes target those parts of the world with the most adverse health outcomes, seeking to protect them against the big-name preventable diseases, such as pneumonia, rotavirus, polio, measles and cholera. As explained on page 146, in 1999, the Gates Foundation pledged $750 million to Gavi, and since then the investment has run into billions, becoming one of the biggest areas of BMGF investment. Its impact on the ground has been profound: 'Our largest immunization grantee is Gavi. From 2000 to 2021, Gavi and its partners immunized nearly 1 billion children, preventing an estimated 15 million deaths.' (BMGF 2023).

We can take the Foundation's efforts in polio eradication as a representative impact study. In 1988, polio was affecting more the 125 countries around the world, paralyzing about 1,000 children every day. Today, following the launch of the Global Polio Eradication Initiative (GPEI) – with the BMGF as a key partner – only two countries (Afghanistan and Pakistan) now record instances of wild polio. In 2020, the World Health Organization (WHO) certified that the whole Africa region was free of wild polio.

Gates' relationship to vaccination work hit new levels of public awareness during the Covid-19 pandemic of 2019–2022. He was a dogged and vocal advocate for the accelerated development and rollout of Covid-19 vaccinations, although he also expressed concerns that the overwhelming focus on this specific disease was hampering routine global immunization programmes for other critical diseases. Given Gates' stature, it was near-inevitable that his drive behind the Covid-19 vaccinations would come in for scrutiny and some adverse analysis. In September 2022, for example, the current affairs website *Politico* published a Special Report entitled 'How Bill Gates and partners used their clout to control the global Covid response — with little oversight' (Banco 2022). In summary, it was critical of the BMGF (and three other global health organizations) for pledging to bridge the equity gap between rich and poor countries, but 'low-income countries were left without life-saving vaccines' (Ibid.). It also claimed that leaders of three of the organizations (including Bill Gates) argued against lifting intellectual property protections on vaccinations that would have helped save lives in the developing world. This was arguably the most serious charge. In April 2022, Gates did indeed oppose a suggested waiver on the World Trade Organization's Agreement on Trade-Related Aspects of Intellectual Property Rights (TRIPS); the waiver would have enforced a temporary suspension of Covid-19-related patents for the duration of the pandemic. But notably, in May 2021, Mark Suzman, then the CEO of the BMGF, announced that the Foundation would actually be supporting the temporary lifting of vaccine patent protections.

To be balanced, Gates is a pragmatist by nature. Anything that might disincentivize the pharmaceutical industry from investing

Personally, Bill Gates has become a lightning rod for conspiracy theorists. Here a protester in London in August 2020 makes wild links between Gates and the Covid pandemic.

the vast amounts of time and money into producing vaccines could, potentially, be disastrously counter-productive. There were also complicated issues surrounding the volume manufacture necessary to counter the pandemic.

Although the Covid-19 threat has firmly receded (at least at the time of writing), Gates is far from complacent about the future. Looking ahead, Gates is confident that the world will be visited by further pandemics, and some could have far greater lethality than Covid-19. In 2022, Gates published a new book, appropriately titled *How to Prevent the Next Pandemic*. In detail, it warns of the threats waiting over the horizon and lays out concrete positions about how the world could gear up its research, science and preparedness to meet those threats, with the optimistic slant that with the right investments Covid-19 could be the world's last pandemic. The book also happens to offer one of the most perfectly succinct and memorable summaries of Gates' relationship to technology and problem-solving: 'I am a technophile. Innovation is my hammer, and I try to use it on every nail I see.' (Gates 2022: n.p.).

The Global Growth and Opportunity Division of the BMGF 'focuses on creating and scaling market-based innovations to stimulate inclusive and sustainable economic growth' (BMGF 2023). It packages its work in five main sub-divisions: Agricultural Development; Financial Services for the Poor; Global Education Program; Nutrition; Water, Sanitation & Hygiene. As the last one on the list clearly demonstrates, BMGF is prepared to tackle some of the least glamorous of social issues. Indeed, Bill Gates has something approaching a personal obsession with the safe disposal and treatment of human sewage, having personally witnessed the appalling impact on human heath of faecal sludge being disposed of directly into the same watercourses that provide the local community with their drinking water.

In 2011, the Foundation initiated the Reinvent the Toilet challenge, throwing down the gauntlet to global engineers to design low-cost toilets that do not require connection to the water supply, electricity grid or sewers. This initiative included a major Reinvented Toilet Expo in 2018 in Beijing, China, in which various toilet designs were demonstrated to Gates and potential manufacturers. Some of these designs are now in action in homes and public spaces around the developing world, changing the lives of those surrounding them. The BMGF also invested heavily in the development of new sewage processing plants, specifically the Omni Processor, a technology that can turn faecal sludge into a biologically harmless material while also producing useful

The Reinvented Toilet Expo in Beijing in November 2018 was the convergence of technological innovation, heavy research funding and Gates' commitment to sanitation in global health.

by-products. One of the most prominent designs in the BMGF portfolio is that produced by Sedron Technologies (formerly Janicki Bioenergy). Through combustion, the Janicki Omni Processor renders the faecal sludge into ash, electricity and potable water – Gates has made several TV appearances in which he drinks and relishes the water that hours before was human excrement. One of the machines was installed in Dakar, Senegal, in 2015 and processes the human waste of up to 100,000 people.

The Global Health Division 'aims to reduce inequities in health by developing new tools and strategies to reduce the burden of infectious disease and the leading causes of child mortality in developing countries' (BMGF 2023). Its job sheet is extensive, and includes Enteric and Diarrheal Diseases, HIV, Innovative Technology Solutions, the Institute for Disease Modeling, Neglected Tropical Diseases, Pneumonia, Tuberculosis and Vaccine Development and Surveillance. One of its more high-profile foci, however, is tackling the global blight of malaria, which kills some 1 million people globally every year. As a press release from 2007 makes clear, the objectives of Bill and Melinda personally in relation to malaria are ambitious: 'Bill and Melinda Gates today called on global leaders to embrace "an audacious goal—to reach a day when no human being has malaria, and no mosquito on earth is carrying it."' (BMGF 2023).

The two remaining divisions within the BMGF are the Global Policy and Advocacy Division and the US Program Division. The former 'seeks to build strategic relationships and promote policies that will help advance our work' (BMGF 2023), with particular focus on Development Policy and Finance, Philanthropic Partnerships and Tobacco Control. The latter is the Foundation's stateside development arm, which includes a heavy leaning towards effective education solutions for K-12 pupils and college students.

As we shall see in the next chapter, Gates places a high premium on education, despite his slightly maverick relationship to it. He has publicly expressed grave concerns about the deficiencies in education for children from low-income homes in the United States, pointing out that if you are born into poverty in the United States you have more chance of going to prison than you have of completing a four-year degree. Through the Foundation, Gates has thought deeply about the metrics for improving educational outcomes, which include: raising the quality of teachers and teaching across the board, with better curriculum support and professional development; focusing on maths as the most important core subject area; reducing racial inequalities in education; providing broader access to IT resources and quality reference materials; and the use of data to refine educational models.

Collectively, the activities of the BMGF can seem almost impossibly ambitious. But returning to the theme of 'giving back', only when we look at what the Foundation is tackling can we appreciate its relationship to Microsoft. Bill Gates made himself the wealthiest man on the planet and Microsoft one of its most profitable companies. Only the years of mono-focused commercial growth made possible the future of Gates' humanitarian and philanthropic work.

CLIMATE CONTROL

Although Bill Gates stepped down from the driving seat of Microsoft some years ago, he has remained a savvy commercial operator, not least in terms of his very extensive investment portfolio.

The BMGF, for example, has major stockholdings in companies such as Berkshire Hathaway Inc. (Warren Buffett's company), Waste Management Inc., Canadian National Railway Company, Caterpillar Inc. and Schrödinger Inc., the total value of these investments in 2022 being somewhere in the region of $19 billion (Edwards 2022). His broad personal share or funding portfolio includes, or has included, automotive retailer AutoNation, aviation manufacturer Eclipse Aviation, the ResearchGate scientific social networking service, EarthNow satellite video broadcaster and Corbis digital image provider. But looking across the full selection of his investments, one theme repeats – the environment.

During the writing of this book, a friend showed me a frothing social media thread she had wandered into. The lead voice had spotted a photograph of aircraft contrails (or 'chemtrails' as the thread defined them) blanketing the sky from horizon to horizon. Whereas most of us might see this as a simple spectacle of the industrial age, the contributor (and many of her contacts) claimed that this was Bill Gates' effort to control the population below through mind-altering chemicals. Apparently, placing a bowl of white wine vinegar outside your house is sufficient to guard against this audacious psychological attack.

As with many conspiracy theories, there can be some very tangential connections to actual truth. While the contrails pictured in the aforementioned thread had nothing to do with Gates and everything to do with normal aircraft engine atmospheric effects, Gates has given financial backing to the Stratospheric Controlled Perturbation Experiment (SCoPEx), launched by Harvard University, which is studying how spraying non-toxic calcium carbonate dust into the atmosphere might potentially offset the effects of global warming. So why is Gates directing his attention to what we call 'geo-engineering'?

In 2021, Gates published another of his landmark books. *How to Avoid Climate Disaster: The Solutions We Have and the Breakthroughs We Need* is an ambitious, data-filled publication underwritten by one unnerving prediction: 'If nothing else changes, the world will keep producing greenhouse gases, climate change will keep getting worse, and the impact on humans will in all likelihood be catastrophic.' (Gates 2021: n.p.). Given that Gates is both informed and usually an optimist, this statement is not hyperbole.

Gates has been researching, or funding researching, into climate change for more than 15 years, giving him a level of expertise possessed by few figures outside of academia. As we might expect, technology offers us some hopeful sunlight through the clouds of possible doom. Gates sees innovation – breakthrough innovation – as our best chance at beating climate change. His funding efforts are therefore directed at a host of high-risk start-ups and industries that might just hold one or several golden keys. As with the BMGF, Gates is focused on broad-spectrum reform, focusing on just about everything that contributes to climate change: the type of materials we use in manufacturing; energy production and consumption; industrial process efficiencies; recycling policies and practices; how to capture carbon from the atmosphere; using geological water pressure to create electrical power; making plant-based meat substitutes (thus reducing our stocks of methane-emitting livestock). No corner of possibility is left unturned.

For Gates, these are far from mere scientific hobbies. Gates is a global leading figure in the fight against climate change. At the

2015 United Nations Climate Change Conference in Paris, Gates was central to the launch of two major programmes – Mission Innovation, an international governmental programme to double research and development (R&D) into carbon-free energy, and Breakthrough Energy, in which major investors could put money into high-risk clean-energy start-ups (Gates himself put $1 billion into this programme).

Gates is aiming high because he sees this level of innovation as the only chance for success. He follows logic where it will. Seeing current green energy solutions (wind, sea, solar etc.) as never quite filling the energy gap, Gates is also one of the major investors in TerraPower, a US company developing the next generation of nuclear reactors – cheaper, more efficient, easy to build, without harmful waste products.

Taken collectively, Gates' investments of global innovation might well, like the Windows-powered PC, shape the world of the future. His visions also might well be constrained by political, social and human factors beyond the powers of technology. But what is clear is that Gates is invested in this world, intellectually, morally and financially, and aims to leave the planet a better place for his descendants.

AFFAIRS OF THE HEART

Gates' philanthropic and humanitarian efforts express the most public-facing side to his character and work. A biography of Gates would, however, be incomplete without including some reflection on his private relationships, at least to the extent that they are impactful on his profile or work. For there are two names in the Bill & Melinda Gates Foundation. Together, Bill and Melinda have formed a partnership for good, as well as spending much of their adult lives together as man and wife. That relationship came to an end in 2021. Some context for why and how this happened is required for a proper understanding of Bill Gates, though I shall guard against sensationalism, reporting only what has been highlighted by the press or offered publicly by both parties.

Given the nearly all-consuming nature of Bill Gates' work ethic across his business career and philanthropic work, it is easy for casual outsiders to sideline the importance of relationships and family in his life. As an unvarnished techie and an uncompromising businessman, Gates is occasionally caricatured as a form of corporate automaton, his brain filled with little but bytes, processes and deals. But this is not the case. Throughout this book, we have nodded towards some of Gates' romantic relationships, not least his lengthy marriage to Melinda. Here, however, we will do a little more digging into those relationships, which form a unique prism through which to see Gates as a more fully rounded character, as problematic as that might be at times.

In his early bachelor years, Gates appeared to possess an undeniably hedonistic side to his personality. James Wallace, in his second part of the Bill Gates story, reported that the youthful Gates had a fondness for riotous parties, including hiring exotic dancers to come round to his Seattle home and swim naked in the pool (Wallace 2011: n.p.). Wallace sees this behaviour as a continuation from his time at Harvard, during which he visited the so-called 'Combat Zone', an area of Boston known for its sex workers, strip clubs and heavy drinking. There were also reports that Gates would hit on attractive female journalists covering Microsoft stories.

Whatever the allegations or the truth behind them, Gates also had some steady girlfriends. The first of these was Jill Bennett, whom Gates met and started dating in 1983. Bennett lived in Seattle and worked as a sales representative for Digital Equipment Corporation (DEC), hence the overlapping worlds that brought her into contact with Gates. Interviewed for *Overdrive*, Bennett remembered Gates as someone having a definite 'sensitive side' and a certain vulnerability that was far from evident in his business dealings. But relationships were tough with someone who was unswervingly dedicated to his business. Bennett explained that Gates operated on the principle of a 'seven-hour turnaround', meaning that he only allowed himself to take seven hours out from Microsoft work in any 24 hours. She even noted that he had removed the radio player from his car so he could devote his driving time to thinking about Microsoft and not be distracted by the entertainment system (Salo 2021).

Understandably, Gates was at this time not an easy option for a long-term relationship. The two separated a short while after, but they remained on close terms as valued friends. From 1991, Bennett began a long struggle against breast cancer, showing her depth of character by becoming a formidable campaigner for cancer research, her efforts including founding the Mary Gates Lectureship Series (a forum for presenting research and support for cancer sufferers) in 2003. Sadly, Bennett died of cancer on 14 July 2014. Gates paid tribute to her shortened but exceptional life: 'She was a remarkable human being—gifted, dedicated, and full of life,' he said. 'She fought her cancer as bravely as anyone I've ever known. She never gave in—she actually found strength in bringing attention to the issue and inspiring people to work toward a cure.' (Salo 2021).

Gates' next significant romantic relationship of the 1980s was with a woman five years his senior, Ann Winblad. Like Gates, Winblad was something of a force to be reckoned with, one indicator of this evaluation being the headline of a 2018 article for morningfuture.com: 'Ann Winblad: the woman who built Silicon Valley' (Morningfuture.com 2018). Winblad was born in Minnesota in 1950 in relatively humble circumstances but went on to take an honours degree in Mathematics and Economics followed by a master's degree in International Economics. She was also a child born to embrace the nascent computer age. At the age of 26, she founded a software development company called Open Systems Inc., also developing a partnership with a hardware company to distribute the software that Open Systems developed. Winblad became an early female success story of the digital revolution, selling her company for $15 million when she was just 32 years old.

Winblad also worked as a consultant for major technology companies, including IBM and Microsoft, and it was during this work that she met and connected with Gates in 1984. The two computer enthusiasts hit it off romantically – they were from the same world and spoke the same language. When they started dating, indeed, Gates' empire was still very much a work in progress. 'Bill wasn't such a big deal when I started dating him,' Winblad recalled to the *San Francisco Chronicle* in 2005. 'And there was a period of time when my net worth was higher than his, and I had to pay for everything. It was a very short period of time, but it was memorable.' (Sheehy 2021).

But it was obvious to Winblad that even though Gates was only 28 when they met, the scale of his ambition was relatively unbounded. In an interview for the *Silicon Valley Business Journal*, she remembered the moment when, during a romantic stroll along a beach, Gates told her that he could see Microsoft's future journey to revenues of $500 million. Bear in mind that at this particular date there had been no software company with revenues hitting even the $100 million mark. This did not seem to dissuade Gates; in fact, the only thing that appeared to concern him was how he was going to take his revenues past the $500 million mark.

Winblad provides other insights into some of the more off-beat corners of Gates' character. In one episode, the pair went away to Mexico for the weekend. Because it was spring break at the time, the pair struggled to find both a hire car and a quality hotel; regarding the former, they had to settle for a dilapidated Volkswagen. But without consulting Winblad, Gates promptly sub-hired the car to a group of teenage boys for $5 a day, asking them to knock on their hotel room door and drop the keys back when they were done. Winblad told Gates that she fully expected the boys not to return the vehicle, to which Gates replied, 'You're probably right.' Nevertheless, the car was returned at 2 o' clock in the morning. As another aside to this trip, Gates' vacation reading was a 1,100-page textbook on molecular biology.

Winblad and Gates dated for a total of three years, breaking up in December 1987. According to Wallace, the break-up occurred at the wedding of Gates' sister Kristi, one of the reported reasons being that the older Winblad was getting ready to settle down at the time, something that Gates wasn't ready to do at that point in his career. As with Bennett, however, the relationship between Gates and Winblad survived and thrived in friendship. In fact, Gates reportedly asked Winblad for her approval for him to marry

Melinda French, the woman who did become his wife. Such was the depth of his relationship with Winblad, even after he was married to Melinda, Bill would meet up for a long friendship weekend with Winblad once a year, ostensibly with Melinda's approval.

In contrast to Winblad, Melinda was nine years younger than Gates. She was born Melinda Ann French on 15 August 1964 in Dallas, Texas, one of four children. Like Gates, she was super bright and an early adopter of computer technology, as a teenager showing an aptitude for computer science and programming. In her higher education, she took a bachelor's degree in Computer Science and Economics from Duke University in 1986, then an MBA from Duke's Fuqua School of Business in 1987.

If ever there was someone ideally suited to Gates, it was Melinda. They met in Microsoft, which hired Melinda as a marketing manager for multimedia products, and began dating in 1988 after meeting at a trade fair in New York. By all accounts, Melinda was (indeed remains) a smart, graceful, self-confident and independent woman, strong in herself and highly capable in her job at Microsoft. According to Wallace, the early years of their relationship 'ran hot and cold', with French apparently aware of Gates' more unrestrained partying (Wallace 1997: n.p.). But after several years of on-off dating, the relationship between the pair intensified and solidified from about 1992. By this time, Gates had a few more years of maturity under his belt and was even beginning to consider the prospect of a wedding, asking married friends for their advice about committed relationships and even including a children's wing in the new luxury home he was building on Lake Washington. He was also on the receiving end of some gentle parental encouragement about settling down.

Gates proposed to Melinda in 1993, and she accepted. She continued to work diligently as a Microsoft manager, refusing to accept any special favours on account of her relationship with the boss. The two were finally married on New Year's Day 1994 in a beautiful beach ceremony on Lanai island, Hawaii. Although the ceremony and the celebrations were by all accounts lavish, with A-list attendees and much dancing on the pure white sands, privacy was a keynote of the event, with the couple's agents doing their best to conceal the date of the wedding from the terrier-like press. Indeed, an insistence on privacy would be a central element of their marriage, as they tried to shield both themselves and eventually their children from press intrusion. The couple would go on to have three children: daughters Jennifer and Phoebe and son Rory.

So 1994 began for Bill Gates with the joy of marriage to a woman he clearly adored. But the year would also bring a tragedy – the death of his mother from cancer on 10 June, at the age of only 64. The passing of Mary Gates was a profound loss for Bill. At the memorial service, he offered a simple, moving insight into the relationship between them: 'I am the son of Mary Gates, and she was a wonderful woman. Not many adult sons are as proud of their mother as I was.' (Wallace 1997: n.p.). Before Mary died, she also left the couple with a gracious admonition to responsibility in a letter sent prior to their marriage: 'From those to whom much has been given, much is expected.'

Bill and Melinda Gates were true to this advice. As a couple running the Bill & Melinda Gates Foundation, they have overseen some of the greatest global philanthropic efforts in modern history. Although the couple regularly attracted press attention, some of it caustic, their high personal profile has never deflected them from delivering on the causes that matter to them.

In 2021, however, the seemingly unthinkable happened when Bill and Melinda Gates announced that they were getting a divorce, ending a relationship that had endured for more than three decades. The divorce was finalized on 21 August. This time, privacy was a scarce commodity, as the press coverage was copious. Public interest was fuelled by the fact that the divorce was not amicable, the separation of ways of two people who had simply grown apart after a long life together. Reports emerged alleging that Gates had had an affair with a Microsoft employee over a long period. Expanding their search, some journalists connected the divorce with Microsoft investigations into the affair in 2020, linking this with Gates' ultimate decision to step down from the Microsoft board. Gates' spokeswoman made an emphatic denial of this claim: 'There was an affair almost 20 years ago which ended amicably. Bill's decision to transition off the board was in no way related to this matter. In fact, he had expressed an interest in spending more time on his philanthropy starting several years earlier?' (Allyn 2021).

Gates did, however, admit to the affair. The press also made wider accusations against Gates regarding what they regarded as womanizing over a period of many years, in both Microsoft and the Bill & Melinda Gates Foundation.

This was clearly a traumatic time for the Gates family, not least because the media was having a field day with the story. Amid all the speculation, Melinda Gates broke with her traditions of personal privacy and did a televised interview with Gayle King on the *CBS Mornings* show. (To date, the interview on YouTube has received 1.8 million views.) She delivered an intimate and clearly emotional insight into the end of the marriage. When asked by King about the root cause of the divorce, Melinda replied: 'It wasn't one moment or one specific thing that happened, there just came a point in time where there was enough there that I realized just wasn't healthy and I couldn't trust what we had.' King then asked Melinda about the reports emerging that Gates had had 'multiple affairs' during their married years. Melinda respectfully answered that, 'You know, I think that those are questions Bill needs to answer.' (*CBS Mornings* 2022).

An additional element to emerge from the interview was Melinda's concern over her husband's relationship with Jeffrey Epstein, the notorious multi-millionaire financier who was convicted of procuring a child for prostitution, then faced further far more serious federal charges of sex trafficking of minors. He cheated facing these charges in court through committing suicide in his prison cell on 10 August 2019. King asked if Gates' relationship with Epstein played any part in her decision to file for divorce: 'Yeah, as I said it's not one thing. It was many things I did not like, that he had had meetings with Jeffrey Epstein. I made that clear to him.' (Ibid.). On one occasion, Melinda actually met Epstein, and came away feeling that he was 'abhorrent, evil personified'. Gates' spokeswoman, Bridgitt Arnold, later issued the following statement: 'Bill Gates regrets ever meeting with Epstein and recognizes it was an error in judgment to do so. Gates recognizes that entertaining Epstein's ideas related to philanthropy gave Epstein an undeserved platform that was at odds with Gates' personal values and the values of his foundation' (Flitter and Stewart 2019).

Bill Gates has understandably been very guarded about the break-up of his marriage, despite repeated attempts of interviewers to draw him on the subject. But in some interviews he has given a few insights revealing the inner impact of the separation and his role in it. During an interview with *Today* in May 2022, for instance, he stated that: 'The divorce is definitely a sad thing. I have responsibility for causing a lot of pain to my family.' When asked directly if he was unfaithful in the marriage he was evasive but sincere: 'I certainly made mistakes and I take responsibility. I don't think delving into the particulars at this point is constructive, but yes, I caused pain, and I feel terrible about that.' (*Today* 2022). By the time he did a substantial interview with Amol Rajan for the BBC, the interview released in February 2023, it was clear the pain was still there, but a reconstruction was clearly beginning. Rajan asked if Gates was still 'grieving' over the divorce, as he had previously stated: 'Well, Melinda's an incredible person, so I'm lucky that I knew her, that we were married. I'm lucky that she still works at the foundation, I'm lucky that we parent our kids, although they are old enough not to need quite as much at this point. You know, there are some regrets but we are moving forward in a very positive way.' (BBC Radio 4 2023).

Gates' life has been characterized by this forward-looking attitude. Looking beyond his personal life, he has used his wealth for good in a way equalled by few other billionaires, and shows no signs of taking his foot off the gas with his humanitarian work. As with Microsoft, for Gates the world itself has become something of a pressing project, a challenge that he is able, intellectually and materially, to tackle.

CHAPTER 6
WHO IS BILL GATES?

Bill Gates is not an easy individual to analyze. The problem is not lack of source material. Bill Gates' life has been massively documented and recorded, every publicly available moment scrutinized in thousands of press articles, countless videos, a decent volume of books (to which library this book contributes) and millions of social media posts and opinions. Indeed, Gates' life has been recorded for posterity to a degree few other individuals experience.

The audiences for these materials are varied. They can be members of the public coming from diverse angles – inspiration, controversy, insight, news. Appropriately, given Gates' career, they might also be tech enthusiasts wanting a critical window into computing's past, with the equal hope that they might glean computing's future. Gates also attracts legions of businesspeople and entrepreneurs, all hoping that some of Gates' magic might rub off on their humbler lives.

But in some ways, it is harder to extract life lessons from Bill Gates than many other high-profile entrepreneurs. Partly this is *because* of the volume of source material – as many historians will attest, getting to the truth can become more complicated the closer to the present day you advance. It is also because Gates is a very private person, or at least one emotionally restrained when under media scrutiny. Watching interviews with Gates, one can be struck by the way he carefully resists opening doors on to his deepest thoughts and feelings. If he does touch on emotions, he seems eager to move on to another topic.

And why not? We have to remember that Gates was born in the 1950s. His generation often have a much less confessional instinct than is characteristic of the present age. But we also gain the impression that to Gates it matters less what you feel and more what you do and what you think. Implicit in our biographical narrative is that Bill Gates is an intensely *pragmatic* and *optimistic* person. His guiding metric is actual impact on the world. That baseline involves looking squarely at reality, developing sound ideas on how to influence that reality, then delivering those ideas with force, propelled by the optimism that action *can* make a difference. In a sense, Gates' life is a demonstration that there is no secret to success, just thought and implementation.

In this chapter, we'll dig a little deeper to extract some life lessons from Bill Gates. The level of his achievement in life, and his daunting intellect, can be intimidating from the outside. But Gates is not the robotic figure sometimes portrayed, rather a fully rounded character whose success has come with as many costs as benefits. He has fought for his success and learned many hard lessons along the way. If anything, Gates illustrates that achievement is as much a matter of finding a sound process and a clearly defined goal and sticking with them.

HOMO SAPIENS DIGITALIS

Bill Gates is at heart a technophile. The bulk of his professional life, even within his humanitarian and philanthropic work, has been driven by the possibilities of technology and science. As a foundational figure behind modern, popular computing, it is unsurprising that Gates sees the world through a digital prism. In Gates' world, if you want success in business or in any enterprise involving widespread impact on the world, you have to understand and embrace technology.

Gates first codified this message in *The Road Ahead*, discussed on page 108. But a later work of greater ambition offers an even more useful data point to unpack Gates' understanding of the interface between business and technology. Gates' landmark business book hit the shelves in 1999. Entitled *Business @ the Speed of Thought: Using a Digital Nervous System*, the book went straight on *The New York Times* bestseller list.

Business @ the Speed of Thought landed at a distinct juncture in the history of global computing. The internet was gaining ground fast, making its presence felt not only in government, business and commerce, but also across many domestic processes, such as shopping and entertainment. At the same time, computers were increasing their power inexorably – processor clock speed accelerated tenfold between 1990 and 2000. At the same time as computers became more relevant, indeed indispensable, to modern life, they also became more affordable, omnipresent in the homes and offices of the developed world. In 1983, there were 12.6 million PCs in the world. By 1990, that number had swelled to 101 million, and in 1999, 435 million. Just six years after Gates published his book, the number of PCs reached 808 million. Gates' book was clearly plugged into the zeitgeist.

The central conceit of *Business @ the Speed of Thought* is what Gates terms the 'digital nervous system' (DNS). The phrase likely did not originate with Gates himself, but to those in the tech industry it became associated with his name more than any other individual. It was a phrase that he had unpacked previously during a speech at Microsoft's Second Annual CEO Summit in 1998:

> The term 'digital nervous system' is kind of an interesting one. The analogy, of course, is to the biological nervous system where you always have the information you need. You always are alert to the most important things, and you block out the information that's not important. And companies really need to have that same kind of thing: the information that's valuable getting to the people who need to know about it.
> (Kelly 1998)

The DNS is about the flow of information, and use and optimization of that information forms the parallel overarching theme within. The opening paragraph of Chapter 1, *Business @ the Speed of Thought*, spells out the importance of competent information handling with absolute conviction:

> I have a simple but strong belief. The most meaningful way to differentiate your company from your competition, the best way to put distance between you and the crowd, is to do an outstanding job with information. *How you gather, manage, and use information will determine whether you win or lose.* There are more competitors. There is more information available about them and about the market, which is now global. The winners will be the ones who develop a world-class digital nervous system so that information can easily flow through their companies for maximum and constant learning.
> (Gates 1999: 4)

In an accelerating world, information is the fuel in the tank. For Gates, the degree to which you are in or out of control of the information flow can determine your success in the present age. Some attitude adjustment is required to develop or tap into the DNS. The title of Chapter 1 is 'Manage with the Force of Facts', which he goes on to explain. First, don't design your business on the basis of desire, drive, ambition or passion. All those qualities are critical for the *delivery* of the business, but if the vision isn't grounded in solid reality it will not gain traction. The second point, building upon the first, is that reality is best accessed through *information*. Only once high-quality information is flowing into and through the business can sound decisions be made, advantages seized, and products designed accurately for the market.

According to Gates, the best way to manage information is by fully embracing digital potentials. *Business @ the Speed of Thought* is a substantial book, nearly 500 pages long in the hardback edition, so there is insufficient space here to list all its content, but we can certainly hit key points.

In the introduction to the book, Gates usefully provides a two-page list of '12 key steps' designed 'to make digital information flow an intrinsic part of your company' (Gates 1999: xx–xxi). Split into three business systems – *knowledge work*, *business operations* and *commerce* – the 12 rules collectively explain how to shift slow, dated analogue processes into rapid digital data management, eliminating tasks that drain time and innovation while also increasing the speed of transactions and the ability to respond to customer needs. By switching to digital processes, the three business systems can be linked together to form the DNS. The rest of the book then squirrels down into the detail of what a DNS really looks like and how it can be constructed and implemented. A persistent theme is that businesses must operate on the basis of *intelligence* in every sense of that word, acquiring deep information about market conditions and possessing the personal and organizational acumen to make bright decisions and innovative leaps.

If we are searching *Business @ the Speed of Thought* for lessons that apply on both the professional and the personal level, Part III of the book – 'Manage Knowledge to Improve Strategic Thought' – is perhaps the most pertinent. It is broken down into six chapters that together form a cogent framework of something approaching a 'Bill Gates method':

Chapter 10   Bad News Must Travel Fast

In a world of exponential change and technological transformation, companies are constantly threatened by the possibility of rapid-onset obsolescence. As a first step to avoiding this, the entire organization, through an optimized DNS, must be primed to identify bad news (i.e. external business threats), share it rapidly and discuss it fearlessly. The last point is assisted by having a 'flatter' corporate hierarchy that encourages open discussion, plus one that rewards 'worthy failure'. We note in passing that although Microsoft certainly did possess something approaching a 'flatter hierarchy' during the early years of its existence, Gates' fiery intolerance of mistakes and slow thinking might not necessarily have encouraged the free flow of information from meeker souls. Ed Roberts of Altair felt that people stopped inviting Gates to meetings because 'he was impossible to deal with' (Wallace & Erickson 1993: 97). But others noticed that he was prepared to accept when he was wrong, indeed those who stood up to him would gain his respect. Steve Wood observed: 'Bill is not dogmatic about things. He's very pragmatic. He can be extremely vocal and persuasive in arguing one side of an issue, and a day or two later he will say he was wrong and let's get on with it. There are not that many people who have the drive and the intensity and the entrepreneurial qualities to be that successful who also have the ability to put their ego aside. That's a rare trait.' (Wallace & Erickson 1993: 128–29).

Chapter 11   Convert Bad News to Good News

In this chapter, Gates encourages his readers to be customer focused with genuine commitment, including being open to adverse feedback, gathered through the information stream of the DNS. The key point is to convert 'bad news' and 'unhappy customers' into genuinely useful learning, insight that is collected, analyzed and alters both policy and product. Certainly, if we look at Gates during the 1980s and 1990s, his levels of customer focus were absolute, ruthlessly overriding the competition to give customers the most appealing and accessible products.

Chapter 12   Know Your Numbers

The DNS should capture and analyze all key business data, all the time. That data is then repurposed to drive every core business decision, from cost control and profit and loss through to marketing and sales. He makes one particularly interesting statement: 'A number on a piece of paper is a dead end; a number in digital form is the start of meaningful thought and action.' (Gates 1999: 221). Gates was at this time highly motivated to convert 'every paper process to a digital process' (Gates 1999: xx). His enthusiasm for the adoption of email during the 1980s, for example, was almost unbounded. In fact, it became borderline problematic as Gates was known to unleash heavy email bombardments on his employees during the early hours of the morning, the numerous messages, often confrontational in tone, greeting the employees as they entered work at what they thought was an early hour. Gates allegedly also used Microsoft's email system to track how hard employees were working by monitoring the times and the days (including weekends) for their email activity.

Chapter 13   Shift People Into Thinking Work
As we have seen, Gates advocates using software and computers to improve and rationalize data collection. But by doing so, the DNS also frees up time for employees to do the type of work that human beings do best, focusing on skills such as decision-making, customer support, marketing and delivery. While Gates is undoubtedly a technophile, this doesn't blind him to the fact that human beings have capabilities beyond the purview of computers.

Chapter 14   Raise Your Corporate IQ
In this chapter, Gates explains how it is crucial for companies to promote knowledge-sharing and to upgrade the intellectual capabilities of their organizations constantly. He argues that once a shared area of knowledge is embedded within a team they should enact it 'with the same unity of purpose and focus as a well-motivated individual' (Gates 1999: 261). To foster the spirit of learning and personal advancement, employees, therefore, should

have immediate access to learning resources, the DNS acting as a pathway to organize and deliver that knowledge.

Chapter 15   Big Wins Require Big Risks

The title of this chapter is self-explanatory. If there is one thing we can certainly say about Bill Gates, he has consistently aimed high throughout his career, free from any trace of self-limiting mindset. Much of this willingness to take the big risks derives from an elevated level of self-belief and personal confidence, but in *Business @ the Speed of Thought* he connects risk-taking with the capabilities of the DNS. In his mind, the 'single biggest way' to achieve major breakthroughs is by managing the accompanying risks with good information derived from data sources and analysis.

Gates sees the effective business sitting perfectly on the interface between digital infrastructure and human intelligence. In the ideal configuration, they are mutually supporting entities, the former providing information flow and adaptive education to the latter, the humans then taking digital knowledge onwards into informed decision. In many ways, Gates also looks at all aspects of business through the eyes of an engineer and programmer. Gates is at heart a rationalist, urging the world to opt into the DNS to compensate for human limitations and maximize human strengths. Given the history of Microsoft during the 2000s, critics might say that Gates did not always practise what he preached. Furthermore, the DNS isn't always the optimal success creator – in volume, data can overload and confuse as much as enlighten. But in our present age, with AI's ever-greater traction over human affairs, the intelligently ordered DNS has never been more relevant.

Gates' organizational thinking is inherently *social* – he recognizes that in business, no man is an island. He has always placed high value on productive human interactions between people of advanced intelligence, reflected in Microsoft's personnel strategies. Microsoft, especially during its growth years, placed a premium on hiring people who brought energy and ideas, but also on technical skills of the highest order. In a 1993 interview, he explained that 'The key for us, number one, has always been hiring very smart people.' For Gates, it was a matter of pure intellectual elitism when it came to the matter of picking people to write software. In fact, he went so far as to saying that 95 per cent of people shouldn't be given responsibility for software coding – only the tip of the personnel iceberg is worthy of the role. But building on this hiring principle, Gates also explained that another key to successful software development was the use of small teams, provided with 'excellent tools' so that they can be powerfully productive. These teams have a high measure of independence; Gates insists that his teams understand 'what they can do to change the spec', resulting in individuals who feel 'very much in control' of the process and the direction. But Gates does not let people riff freely on a theme. He explains that the process should also include having 'lots of people read the code' to avoid a situation in which one person 'is kind of hiding the fact that they can't solve a problem' (Gates 1993). Every process, every line of code, should be under a strong spotlight, with nowhere for erroneous or sloppy thinking to conceal itself.

In the same interview, Gates also explained that when it came to developing software, 'Source code itself is where you should put all your thoughts, not in any other thing.' There is something of a Zen-like mysticism infusing this statement, the sense that the programmer should be so focused on the code that all other considerations fall away. There is a fusion of pragmatism and creativity here. Computer code has an unwavering relationship with reality, in that it either functions properly or it doesn't, but a good programmer has a certain degree of artistry, striving for a simple beauty in their code. Productive code, not abstract methodology, is where the real work is done. Essentially, he is urging us to define the most important thing and get to work on it.

THE SUCCESS MODE

In a 1984 interview with CNBC, Bill Gates appeared utterly comfortable with his own brilliance and success. He looked poised and at ease. Interviewer Jane Pauley probed behind the confident front. She asked the still-young entrepreneur about whether he might see himself eventually working for someone else: 'I never have. I'm used to working for a company where the ideas that I have are something that I can easily pursue, so I think it would be a tough transition.' Gates was evidently enjoying being at the tip of the spear. A psychologically interesting moment came when Pauley referenced the fact that people called Gates a 'genius'. Expecting a humble pushback from Gates that did not come, Pauley observed that 'I don't think that embarrassed you at all'. She went on to ask him whether he was indeed a 'business genius', in addition to his evident prowess in computing: 'Well, I wouldn't say "genius". I enjoy working with the people and talking about what we are going to get done, getting real excited, making sure that the structure is there, and that the ideas get measured properly. And really leading the company … that's exciting.'

It was clear from this response that Gates was both highly motivated and, equally, deeply analytical. Gates was no robotic nerd; here was an individual with genuine passion and drive. Pauley queried whether Gates was worried that he might burn out from the effort of it all. His response was unequivocal: 'No. The work we are doing ... it's not like we are doing the same thing all day long. We go into our offices and think up new programs, we get together in meetings, we go out and see end users, we talk to customers. There's so much variety and there's always new things going on. I don't think there will ever come a time when that will become boring.' (*CNBC Make It* 2019).

Although this interview came relatively early in Bill Gates' career, its underlying ideas still marry closely with the enthusiasm and processes that Gates has drawn on to this day. For those wanting to extract lessons here, there are some nuggets of gold easily picked off the surface. Gates' intellectual stamina and unrivalled work ethic are sustained by a burning motivation, renewed on a daily basis, to succeed. But he also suggests that the flames of motivation can be fanned by the very structure of daily work experience. He promotes, for example, the benefits of variety in working life, frequent task-switching preventing the work from becoming 'boring' – he appears to connect burn-out with the rote performance of repetitive duties over time. He also places a value upon human interaction, either internal to the company or external with the customer, as a way to energize thinking and to keep stimulus at a high level. If there is a message to extract here, it might simply be that if we want to have energy for our work, we need to approach that work in an energetic way, and let the dynamism of the day generate our motivation.

At the individual level, intelligence is crucial to Gates. Much of his reputation derives from his exceptional mental acuity, many first-hand observers acknowledging that he is generally the brightest person in the room, often by a long measure. There must surely be a powerful genetic component to his intelligence, but this is given a turbo-drive by Gates' general love of learning. Here Mike Slade, a former marketing director at Microsoft, explains Gates' formidable educational drive plus his enviable abilities for retention of information:

> He is joyous about learning things, like no-one I've ever met in my life. He doesn't read one book about something he'll read, like, five books about something, most of which are too dense for any mortal to read. And he reads really fast and synthesizes really well. The most amazing thing is he almost always knows more than the other person he is talking to about whatever it is. It's unbelievable. (Netflix 2018)

Bernie Noe, a friend of his, noted that when they went away on holiday, Gates read something like 14 books at a rate of 150 pages per hour with a 90 per cent retention rate, which Noe acknowledged was 'kind of extraordinary' (Ibid.).

Clearly, Gates is the embodiment of the phrase 'leaders are readers'. For him, the diligent reading of books is an act of continual empowerment. Gates has likened reading informative, well-written and well-argued books as akin to having your very own hot-shot line-up of personal tutors, the whole world of information and ideas at your fingertips. Owning the books, however, has no value in itself – Gates forcefully urges us to make time to actually read, digest and understand them, explicating some of his personal reading rules during an interview: 'I don't let myself start a book that I'm not going to finish. [...] If you are reading books such as these [demanding non-fiction works] then you want to be sitting down for an hour at a time – you want to get your mind around it, it's not the kind of thing you can do five minutes here or ten minutes there. Magazine articles fit, YouTube videos fit, into those little slots. So every night I'm reading for a little over an hour.' (Quartz 2017).

During the hour of close study, Gates is not a passive reader. He sees books as living objects requiring an active-reading strategy. Good note-making is one of the approaches he applies to reading, even though there is clearly a cost in energy and time: 'When you are reading you have to be careful that you really are concentrating, particularly if it's a non-fiction book. You take in the new knowledge and you attach it to knowledge you have. For me, taking notes ensures that I'm really thinking hard about what's in there. If I disagree with the book, sometimes it takes a long time for me to read the book because I'm writing so much in the margins. It's actually kind of frustrating – oh, please say something I agree with so I can get through to the end.' (Ibid.).

Interestingly, given his predilection for digital information, Gates also explains that he likes using traditional printed books and articles, even though he has an entire library of e-content on various devices. He explains this in terms of personal preference, but he has the weight of modern science behind him – recent research on the act of reading has shown that reading on paper has significant advantages in concentration and retention of information when compared to electronic text. Being a physical object, with dimensions, borders and a text flow divided between pages, printed books provide a physical framework for locating and understanding information, as opposed to the free-streaming content of an ebook.

For intellectual development, Gates clearly recommends the spaciousness of undistracted reading. One distinctive practice he applies to accelerate his learning is the self-investment of biannual 'think weeks'. A think week consists of a seven-day period in which Gates takes himself to a remote location, typically a rural log cabin with little or no connectivity. There, he spends every day reading voraciously without interruption on an important subject, finding the space and time to acquire new knowledge and turn the subject over carefully in his mind. He also uses the opportunity to consider future directions.

Note that this is not a casual reading holiday – Gates can spend up to 18 hours of every day reading demanding new content. But 'think weeks' have had an important influence on his career. His 1995 internal memo 'The Internet Tidal Wave', which gave power to the production of Internet Explorer, was itself the product of think-week activity. According to a *Wall Street Journal* report, other think-week outputs include plans to develop Microsoft's version of the tablet PC, greater security in software applications and the pursuit of online video gaming (Guth 2005). https://www. wsj.com/articles/SB111196625830690477).

Gates is something of a poster child for lifelong learning. He never stops acquiring knowledge in new fields of interest, but typically loops whatever fresh knowledge is acquired back into his practical endeavours. Not unsurprisingly, he places a high value on education, and takes frequent courses to top up his learning. But for Gates, education does not need to be formal, it just needs to be committed and structured. Knowledge for its own sake, or worse, acquired purely for the purposes of social status, is empty learning. The best form of educational output is to channel knowledge into tackling big issues of social importance. This belief in the responsibility that comes with knowledge is evident in a 2007 commencement address that Gates delivered at Harvard University, returning to the alma mater from which he never graduated. He brought the address to a rousing climax as he exhorted a mostly young audience to find a focus, stick with it, and make a difference:

> In line with the promise of this age, I want to exhort each of the graduates here to take on an issue, a complex problem, a deep inequity and become a specialist on it. If you make it the focus of your career that would be phenomenal. But you don't have to do that to make an impact. For a few hours every week you can use the growing power of the internet to get informed, find others with the same interests, see the barriers and find ways to cut through them. Don't let complexity stop you. Be activists. Take on big inequities. I feel sure it will be one of the great experiences of your lives.
>
> You graduates are coming of age at an amazing time. As you leave Harvard you have technology that members of my class never had. You have awareness of global inequity which we did not have. And with that awareness, you likely also have an informed conscience that will torment you if you abandon these people whose lives you could change with modest effort. You have more than we had, you must start sooner and carry on longer.
>
> And I hope you will come back here to Harvard 30 years from

now and reflect what you have done with your talent and your energy.

I hope you will judge yourselves not on your professional accomplishments alone, but also on how well you have addressed the world's deepest inequities. On how well you treated people a world away, who have nothing in common with you but their humanity.

Good luck.

(Harvard University 2013)

'Don't let complexity stop you.' Looking back over the daunting convolutions of Microsoft's history, Gates is doubtless aware that if most of us could see the twists and turns of our futures in advance we might be put off tackling many of our most important endeavours. Simply committing to the project in hand initiates the process of breaking down complexity into digestible steps, eventually bringing a sense of clarity and control. In the address, Gates also clearly sees a sense of obligation in the potential of every life, not least because our future self will ultimately look back and pass judgement on our historical self.

Gates also advocates realism in checking our own performance. We have already seen this principle at work in the DNS, where computerization provides the data and information without which our thinking becomes disconnected from reality. In a Bloomberg interview, Gates fleshes out the idea of self-measurement, giving a concrete illustration from his work in international disease control:

I think the quality that has helped me in lots of things is a kind of measurement, scientific framework, where I go in and say 'Did

anybody handle this well, what are the very best practices? Do we have numbers on that?' And let's get everyone measuring what they are doing so they can strive to match what that best achievement is. For us, often, that's something like getting the vaccines out to all the children. Some very poor countries do that extremely well because they get down to that local level and measure the activity. They make sure the inventory is there, they make sure the workers are showing up. So for me I always look at how can we do better measurement and use that to drive the very best practices.
(Bloomberg Originals 2016)

This quotation brings to mind the 'Know the Numbers' theme in *Business @ the Speed of Thought*. Just wishing for something to happen does not make it so, or at least does not make it successful. In Gates' worldview, businesses and individuals must constantly run background checks on their ideas, showing that they have a tangible or quantifiable connection with real-world effects.

Regardless of the good idea, even one atop a mountain of confirmatory data, little will be achieved without the application of hard work. An astonishing work ethic has been a key ingredient in Gates' recipe for success. In Microsoft, he had an unrelenting attitude to grinding the hours. Other members of staff regularly found him passed out beneath the desk, sleeping like a child after a marathon programming session. The concepts of regular daily breaks and – God forbid – days off were anathema to Gates for many years. Such commitment brought outstanding productivity. More problematically, however, Gates has since recognized that he could impose his work ethic on to others and expect them to meet his own impossible standards of labour fanaticism. During his early years at Microsoft, for example, he would memorize the number plates of all the staff cars in the car park so he would be able to monitor who was present and who was not. Consequently, Microsoft staff were under the constant pressure of presenteeism – some individuals might even sleep at the office to ensure that their car was visible when the boss arrived at work. Gates has since admitted, in an interview for the BBC's *Desert Island Discs*, that time gave him a little more perspective: 'Eventually I had to loosen up as the company got to a reasonable size.' (Robertson 2016).

Gates' frankly terrifying working hours are not atypical of hyper-successful entrepreneurs. The ability to deliver very long hours productively is a common characteristic of history's high achievers, especially if that individual can retain rationality and

Few entrepreneurs had had such historical sociopolitical impact as Bill Gates. Here he stands aside the German Chancellor Angela Merkel at a reception in Berlin in January 2008.

self-control across an 80-plus-hour working week. In interviews, Gates has acknowledged his passion for work, but in more recent years he has also accepted that motivations change over time. A particularly fascinating interview with Gates was hosted by none other than his own father, conducted on stage in New York on 2 June 2010. At one point, the conversation revolved around arguments made by Canadian journalist and author Malcolm Gladwell, who analyzed the theory that it takes roughly 10,000 hours of practice to become expert in anything. (Gladwell made this critique in his 2008 book *Outliers: The Story of Success*, a work that also included interviews with Gates.) At the same time, Gladwell acknowledged that success could also involve a large measure of fortunate timing. Gates fine-tuned his response by acknowledging the roles of luck and historical moment in his achievements, but also a form of statistical survivor bias:

His book makes a lot of great points, that is, that in all success stories there are significant elements of luck and timing. You know, I wasn't the only kid born between 1953 and 1955. But absolutely, to be young and open-minded at a time when the microprocessor was invented… [...] If somebody reads the book to say that if you spend 10,000 hours doing something you'll be super-good at it – I don't think it's as simple as that. What you do is about 50 hours, and about 90 per cent drop out of it because they don't like it or they're not good [at it]. You know, you do another 50 hours and about 90 per cent drop out. So there are these constant cycles. And you do have to be lucky enough but also fanatical enough to keep going. And so the person who makes it to the 10,000 hours is not just somebody who's done it for 10,000 hours. They are somebody who has chosen and been chosen in many different times. And so all these magical things came together, including who I knew at that time. And I think, you know, that's very important. When you look at somebody who is good and say, 'Could I do it like them?' they've gone through so many cycles that it might fool you. Yes you could, with the right luck and imagination and some talent. (Fora.tv 2011)

Gates' view on what it takes to be a success contains his typical fusion of restrained optimism and practical realism. To reach a lofty end goal in any field of endeavour needs, unless you have lottery-winning luck on your side, 'fanatical' persistence to keep going through endless cycles of testing and challenge. Success is like an elite endurance event, each demanding stage of the race weeding out those who are unfit to continue until only a few winners are left to cross the finish line. But for those who can endure, the rewards are there.

Bill Gates is not a simple role model for those wanting a mentor on the road to success. Nor does he offer an easy formula to apply to a complex world. His life in business has been an exercise in crossing thousands of obstacles, great and small, human and inanimate, digital and analogue, that have been scattered across his path. Gates' secret to success (if it is not too portentous to call it that) is actually quite straightforward – he maintains *intelligent* pressure on the problem at hand, progressively and repeatedly performing actions that maximize the possibility, not the guarantee, of success.

CONCLUSION

At the very end of *Business @ the Speed of Thought*, Bill Gates pulls together the threads of his vision of the future. In the years ahead, he sees towering opportunities for advancement and success, alongside unforgiving threats to unwary, slow or complacent companies. It includes, however, an overarching statement that in many ways gets to the heart of Gates' personality: 'I am an optimist. I believe in progress. I'd much rather be alive today than at any time in history – and not just because in an earlier age my skill set wouldn't have been as valuable and I'd have been a prime candidate for some beast's dinner. The tools of the Industrial Age extended the capabilities of our muscles. The tools of the digital age extend the capabilities of our minds. I'm even happier for my children, who will come of age in this new world.' (Gates 1999: 413–14). Given some of the problems our planet has faced since 1999, Gates' positivity might appear more as historical naivety. Time has marched on and some of the gloss has rubbed off the digital world, with grave concerns about the effects of unbridled internet freedom on mental health, global security, information, privacy and politics.

But Bill Gates is different to most of us. He has *personally* and successfully engineered global change through the work of his own hands and teams. He *knows* that big work, great results, can be achieved if you apply your mind and resources. Optimism would be unwarranted if change were impossible. Gates knows that that change is possible on every level.

Certainly, his optimism seems to have endured over time. In 2008, nearly a decade after he published *Business @ the Speed of Thought*, Gates reiterated his sunny-side-up position at the World Economic Forum:

> Let me begin by expressing a view that some do not share: The world is getting better, a lot better. In significant and far-reaching ways, the world is a better place to live than it has ever been. Consider the status of women and minorities in society – virtually any society compared to any time in the past. Consider that life expectancy has nearly doubled during the last 100 years. Consider governance, the number of people today who vote in elections, express their views, and enjoy economic freedom compared to any time in the past. In many crucial areas, the world is getting better. These improvements have been triggered by advances in science, technology, and medicine. They have brought us to a high point in human welfare. We're really just at the becoming of this technology-driven revolution in what people can do for one another. In the coming decades, we'll have astonishing new abilities: better software, better diagnosis for illness, better cures, better education, better opportunities and more brilliant minds coming up with ideas that solve tough problems. This is how I see the world, and it should make one thing clear: I am an optimist.
>
> But I am an impatient optimist. The world is getting better, but it's not getting better fast enough, and it's not getting better for everyone.
>
> (World Economic Forum 2008)

The 'impatient optimist'. These two words perfectly capture Gates' restlessness with the status quo and belief he can shape things for the better. Even after the end of his marriage, an event that we sense has cut him very deeply, his default is to stay future-oriented, actively seeking the means to bring about change and move ahead on the upbeat.

Is there anything that unsettles Bill Gates' optimism, not least in relation to technology? Way back in 1993, Gates reflected on the emergent possibilities of artificial intelligence, explaining that 'if you look out far enough the computer will eventually learn to reason in somewhat the same way that humans do' (Gates 1993). This, he admitted, was 'a little scary'.

He was foreshadowing not merely the Large Language Models (LLMs) that are already having profound impact, but rather 'artificial general intelligence' (AGI), which has recently prompted the likes of Elon Musk and Steve Wozniak to call for a six-month moratorium on AI development. Machine-learning expert Eliezer Yudkowsky goes further, proposing that we close down major AI servers and literally bomb those that don't, such are the risks to humanity in the rise of a super-AI. Yudkowsky has been most explicit by stating: 'The most likely result of building a superhumanly smart AI, under anything remotely like the current circumstances, is that literally everyone on Earth will die.' (Yudkowsky 2023).

Today's Bill Gates is certainly less confident about AI's benefits. Asked by ABC News' Rebecca Jarvis whether he is scared about AI, he responded: 'We are all scared that a bad guy could grab it. Let's say the bad guys get ahead of the good guys. Then something like cyberattacks could be driven by an AI.' But he stops well short of saying that AI research should be put on pause: 'If you just pause the good guys and you don't pause everyone else you are probably hurting yourself. You definitely want the good guys to have strong AI.' (ABC News 2023). Gates' resistance to government restraints on technological progress remind us of his defence against attempts to contain and cut up Microsoft in the 1990s and 2000s. Technological evolution is for Gates as relentless and unstoppable as water; what matters is that the 'good guys' win.

Gates has given another, more intimate, answer to the question 'What scares you?' during the three-part Netflix documentary *Inside Bill's Brain: Decoding Bill Gates*. When asked this question, he paused for a considered reply, then explained his biggest fear is that his brain will 'stop working'. Bill Gates has, ultimately, forged his success via the supercomputer in his head, regardless of how much assistance he has had from digital devices. As he advances through his 60s, his continuing impatience to get things done might simply be a reflection that time and opportunity do not run on indefinitely.

In another interview with Amol Rajan for the BBC, released on 3 February 2023, Gates was asked a question that surely intrigues us all. Rajan noted that Swedish environmental activist Greta Thunberg credited her Asperger's Syndrome as her 'superpower', and enquired whether Gates felt that he also possessed a superpower: 'You know I think I'm a student, I'm curious. [...] My ability to concentrate is *very* high, and when I was young it was weirdly high, you know, to memorize things and to try out my thinking, which made science and math super-interesting. Then I discovered software and I was able to throw all my energy into that. So I'm a good student I think.' (BBC Radio 4 2023).

Amol pushed further. He enquired whether Gates had 'an unusual ability to focus on a task at hand' – Gates simply replied 'Yes'. Amol followed up by asking whether Gates had something of a 'Gatsby complex', referring to the ambiguous super-rich central character in F. Scott Fitzgerald's novel *The Great Gatsby*. Gates explained that there was a quotation from Gatsby displayed in his library in his home: 'His dream must have seemed so close, that he could hardly fail to grasp it.' Amol wondered whether Gates had achieved his (American) dream: 'I certainly feel that I have fulfilled most of my goals. I have enough left to keep me busy. But you know I'm incredibly lucky. I had my Microsoft career, I have amazing kids, I have my foundation career, I'm healthy, I've got great friends. You know, I'm as lucky a person as is living.' (Ibid.). Whatever status Gates has in modern human history – and that is considerable – he ultimately appreciates that he has been a fortunate man.

BIBLIOGRAPHY

BOOKS AND ARTICLES

Afil, Raphael (2021). *Bill Gates: In His Own Words*.

Allen, Paul (2012). *Idea Man: A Memoir by the Co-founder of Microsoft*. Kindle Edition. London: Penguin.

Allyn, Bobby (16 May 2021). 'Microsoft Board Investigated Bill Gates' "Intimate Relationship' With Employee". *NPR*: https://www.npr.org/2021/05/16/997363526/microsoft-board-investigated-bill-gates-intimate-relationship-with-employee

Apple-Microsoft (1985). 'Text of Apple-Microsoft Agreement': https://www.tech-insider.org/windows/research/1985/1122.html

Arnett, Nick, and Scott Palmer (28 March 1988). 'Gates Challenges Apple Copyright Claims, Citing Licensing Agreement'. *InfoWorld: The PC News Weekly*: viewed via Google Books.

Banco, Erin and Ashleigh Furlong and Lennart Pfahler (14 September 2022). 'How Bill Gates and partners used their clout to control the global Covid response—with little oversight'. *Politico*: https://www.politico.com/news/2022/09/14/global-covid-pandemic-response-bill-gates-partners-00053969

Bill & Melinda Gates Foundation (BMGF) – pages accessed 2023:
– https://www.gatesfoundation.org/ideas/media-center/press-releases/1997/06/bill-and-melinda-gates-establish-library-foundation
– https://www.gatesfoundation.org/our-work#program_strategies
– https://www.gatesfoundation.org/our-work#program_strategies
– https://www.gatesfoundation.org/our-work/programs/global-development/immunization
– https://www.gatesfoundation.org/our-work
– https://www.gatesfoundation.org/ideas/media-center/press-releases/2007/10/chart-a-course-for-malaria-eradication
– https://www.gatesfoundation.org/our-work#program_strategies

Department of Justice (1999). *United States of America (Plaintive) vs. Microsoft Corporation (Defendant)*, Civil Action No. 98-1232 (TPJ): https://www.

justice.gov/sites/default/files/atr/legacy/2006/04/11/msjudge.pdf

Dudley, Brier (31 July 2008). 'Microsoft's "Mama" dies; first office manager helped company grow up'. *The Seattle Times*: https://www.seattletimes.com/business/microsofts-mama-dies-first-office-manager-helped-company-grow-up/Duncan, Ray (General Editor) (1988). *The MS-DOS Encyclopedia*. Redmond, WA: Microsoft Press.

Edwards, John (27 December 2022). 'This Is What Bill Gates' Portfolio Looks Like'. Investopedia.com: https://www.investopedia.com/articles/markets/101215/what-bill-gatess-portfolio-looks.asp

Flitter, Emily and James B. Stewart (12 October 2019). 'Bill Gates Met With Jeffrey Epstein Many Times, Despite His Past'. *The New York Times*: https://www.nytimes.com/2019/10/12/business/jeffrey-epstein-bill-gates.html

Forbes (13 January 2000). 'Gates Steps Down As Microsoft CEO': https://www.forbes.com/2000/01/13/mu7.html

Fox, Emily Jane (4 November 2016). 'How Bill Gates and Steve Ballmer's Bromance Fell Apart'. *Vanity Fair*: https://www.vanityfair.com/news/2016/11/steve-ballmer-bill-gates-friendship

Gammon, Katharine (19 May 2008). 'What We'll Miss About Bill Gates—a Very Long Good-Bye'. *Wired*: https://www.wired.com/2008/05/st-billgates/

Gates, Bill (31 January 1976). 'An Open Letter to Hobbyists'. *Homebrew Computer Club Newsletter*, volume 2, issue 1.

Gates, Bill (1993). 'Bill Gates Interview'. National Museum of American History, Smithsonian Institution: https://americanhistory.si.edu/comphist/gates.htm

Gates, Bill (1995). 'The Internet Tidal Wave'. Quoted in *Wired* (26 May 2010). 'May 26, 1995: Gates, Microsoft Jump on "Internet Tidal Wave"': https://www.wired.com/2010/05/0526bill-gates-internet-memo/

Gates, Bill with Nathan Myhrvold and Peter Rinearson (1996). *The Road Ahead*. New York: Viking Penguin.

Gates, Bill (2001). *Business @ the Speed of Thought: Using a Digital Nervous System*. New York City: Warner Books.

Gates, Bill and Melinda (2010): The Giving Pledge Letter: https://givingpledge.org/foundingletter

Gates, Bill and Rashida Jones (23 November 2020). 'Bill

Gates and Rashida Jones Ask Big Questions': https://new-media.gatesnotes.com/media/GN_Media/media/Files/PodcastBillGatesandRashidaJonesAskBigQuestionsepisode02transcript.pdf

Gates, Bill (2021). *How to Avoid Climate Disaster: The Solutions We Have and the Breakthroughs We Need*. London: Allen Lane.

Gates, Bill (2022). *How to Prevent the Next Pandemic*. London: Allen Lane.

Gladwell, Malcolm (2009). *Outliers: The Story of Success*. London: Penguin.

Good, Dan (2020). *The Microsoft Story: How the Tech Giant Rebooted its Culture, Upgraded its Strategy, and Found Success in the Cloud*. New York: HarperCollins.

Goodell, Jeff (13 March 2014). 'Bill Gates: The *Rolling Stone* Interview. The richest man in the world explains how to save the planet'. *Rolling Stone*: https://www.rollingstone.com/culture/culture-news/bill-gates-the-rolling-stone-interview-111915/?print=true

Guth, Robert (28 March 2005). 'In Secret Hideaway, Bill Gates Ponders Microsoft's Future'. *The Wall Street Journal*: https://www.wsj.com/articles/SB111196625830690477

Guth, Robert A. (5 June 2008). 'Gates-Ballmer Clash Shaped Microsoft's Coming Handover'. *The Wall Street Journal*: https://www.wsj.com/articles/SB121261241035146237?mod=googlenews_wsj&apl=y&r=125394

Huddleston, Tom (29 January 2020). 'Bill Gates calls Apple's first Mac a "great machine" in this 1983 internal video'. CNBC: https://www.cnbc.com/2020/01/29/video-bill-gates-steve-jobs-in-1983-internal-apple-promo-video.html

Isaacson, Walter (2011). *Steve Jobs: The Exclusive Biography*. London: Hachette Digital.

Johnston, Stuart J. (24 September 1990). 'IBM/Microsoft Reassess OS/2 Partnership'. *InfoWorld: The PC News Weekly,* 1, 121: viewed via Google Books.

Kastrenakes, Jacob (4 February 2014). 'Bill Gates to "substantially increase time" at Microsoft after stepping down as chairman'. Theverge.com: https://www.theverge.com/2014/2/4/5377226/bill-gates-steps-down-microsoft-chairman-named-tech-advisor

Kelly, Kevin (1998). 'The Digital Nervous System: Technology that responds to a changing marketplace'. *The Rough Notes Magazine*: https://roughnotes.com/rnmagazine/1998/october98/10p34.htm

Lammers, Susan (1990). *Programmers at Work: Interviews with 19 Programmers Who Shaped the Computer Industry*. Seattle: Microsoft Press.

Maher, Jimmy (31 July 2017). 'The complete history of the IBM PC, part two: The DOS empire strikes'. Arstechnica.com: https://arstechnica.com/gadgets/2017/07/ibm-pc-history-part-2/

Manes, Stephen & Paul Andrews (2013). *Gates: How Microsoft's Mogul Reinvented an Industry—and Made Himself the Richest Man in America*. Cadwallader & Stern. Kindle Edition.

Microsoft (15 June 2006). 'Microsoft Announces Plans for July 2008 Transition for Bill Gates': https://news.microsoft.com/2006/06/15/microsoft-announces-plans-for-july-2008-transition-for-bill-gates/

Microsoft (2007). 'Bill Gates: United Kingdom Launch of Windows Vista and 2007 Microsoft Office System at the British Library': https://news.microsoft.com/2007/01/31/bill-gates-united-kingdom-launch-of-windows-vista-and-2007-microsoft-office-system-at-the-british-library/

Microsoft/Sony (7 April 1998). 'Microsoft and Sony to Collaborate in Creating the Convergence of Personal Computer, Digital Television and Consumer Audio-Visual Platforms': https://www.sony.com/en/SonyInfo/News/Press_Archive/199804/98-0408/

Mohr, Ian (17 May 2021). 'Melinda Gates could be angling to change kids' $10M inheritance in split'. Foxbusiness.com: https://www.foxbusiness.com/lifestyle/bill-melinda-gates-kids-inheritance-split

Morningfuture.com (2018). 'Ann Winblad: the woman who built Silicon Valley': https://www.morningfuture.com/en/2018/07/13/annwinblad-silicon-valley-venture-capitalist-investor-women-startup/

Neuborne, Ellen (19 November 1998). 'Microsoft's Teflon Bill'. *Bloomberg Businessweek*: http://www.businessweek.com/1998/48/b3606125.htm

Reference for Business (2023). 'Bill & Melinda Gates Foundation – Company Profile, Information, Business Description, History, Background Information on Bill & Melinda Gates Foundation': https://www.referenceforbusiness.com/history2/16/Bill-Melinda-Gates-Foundation.html

Robertson, Alexander (31 January 2016). 'Bill Gates memorised his employees' number plates so he could keep tabs on when they were turning up for work'. *Daily Mail*: https://www.dailymail.co.uk/news/article-3425080/Bill-Gates-memorised-employees-number-plates-tabs-turning-work.html

Rojas, Peter (2 May 2005). 'The Endgadget Interview: Bill Gates, Part 1'. Endgadget.com: https://www.engadget.com/2005-05-02-the-engadget-interview-bill-gates-part-1.html?guccounter=1

Rushe, Dominic (30 March 2011). 'Microsoft co-founder lays bare his battles with Bill Gates.' *The Guardian*: https://www.theguardian.com/technology/2011/mar/30/microsoft-paul-allen-bill-gates

Salo, Jackie (20 May 2021). 'Bill Gates' dating history: From Ann Winblad to Melinda Gates'. *New York Post*: https://nypost.com/article/bill-gates-dating-history-girlfriends/

Scoglio, Chris (2 April 2018). 'The Evolution of the Xbox'. Medium.com: https://medium.com/@cscoglio/the-ups-and-down-s-of-the-xbox-creation-2959bb2f4050

Scipioni, Jade (24 June 2019). 'Bill Gates reveals his "greatest mistake" that potentially cost Microsoft $400 billion'. CNBC.com: https://www.cnbc.com/2019/06/24/bill-gates-says-his-biggest-mistake-was-not-beating-google-on-android.html

Sheehy, Kate (4 May 2021). 'Bill Gates took getaways with his ex-girlfriend after marriage to Melinda.' *The New York Post*: https://nypost.com/2021/05/04/bill-gates-took-getaways-with-old-girlfriend-after-marriage/US Court of Appeals, Ninth Circuit (19 September 1994). *Apple Computer, Inc. v. Microsoft Corp.* 35 F.3d 1435, 1442 (9th Cir. 1994): https://law.justia.com/cases/federal/appellate-courts/F3/35/1435/605245/

Van Dam, Andrew (9 October 2019). 'It's better to be born rich than gifted.' *The Washington Post*: https://www.washingtonpost.com/business/2018/10/09/its-better-be-born-rich-than-talented/?noredirect=on

Wallace, James & Jim Erickson (1992). *Hard Drive: Bill Gates and the Making of the Microsoft Empire*. New York: HarperBusiness.

Wallace, James (1997). *Overdrive: Bill Gates and the Race to Control Cyberspace*. Kindle Edition. Hoboken, NJ: John Wiley & Sons.

Yudkowsky, Eliezer (29 March 2023). 'Pausing AI Developments Isn't Enough. We Need to Shut it All Down'. *Time*: https://time.com/6266923/ai-eliezer-yudkowsky-open-letter-not-enough/

SOCIAL MEDIA

Chapter 1

Bill Gates (2020): https://www.linkedin.com/posts/williamhgates_
remembering-my-father-activity-6711757743981658112-g55f/?trk=public_
profile_like_view

Bill Gates (15 September 2020). 'Remembering my father'. GatesNotes:
The blog of Bill Gates: https://www.gatesnotes.com/Remembering-Bill-
Gates-Sr?WT.mc_id=20200915000000_Remembering-Bill-Gates-Sr_BG-
LI_&WT.tsrc=BGLI

Chapter 3

Bill Gates (6 October 2011). 'Remembering Steve Jobs'. GatesNotes: The blog
of Bill Gates: https://www.gatesnotes.com/Steve-Jobs

Chapter 5

Bill Gates (13 July 2022). Twitter: https://twitter.com/BillGates/
status/154723538859
4331648

VIDEOS

Chapter 1

Netflix (2018). *Inside Bill's Brain: Decoding Bill Gates*: https://www.netflix.
com/gb/title/80184771

Bill Gates (2010). 'Bill Gates reflects on his school life'. The Financial Review:
https://www.youtube.com/watch?v=6mFM3Q8c
Wm0&t=336s

Chapter 2

Bill Gates (1984). 'Bill Gates Wasn't Worried About Burnout In 1984 – Here's
Why'. *CNBC Make It* (26 February 2019): https://www.youtube.com/
watch?v=MhnSzwXvGfc

Chapter 3

Raikes, Jeff (2010). *The Jeff Raikes Story: Part Two*. Microsoft Developer
Network Channel 9: channel9.msdn.com/series/history/the-history-of-
microsoft-the-jeff-raikes-story-part-two

Bill Gates (1987). 'Computer History: Rare Talk – Bill Gates on Competition,
Lotus, IBM and the future of Microsoft 1987.' Computer History

Archives Project (CHAP) (24 July 2021): https://www.youtube.com/watch?v=BXGJEHEj-KA

Bill Gates (1983). '1983 Apple Macintosh Dating Game'. Factorx801: https://www.youtube.com/watch?v=5J3FUOCRXPo

Microsoft (8 April 2010). 'The History of Microsoft – The Jeff Raikes Story: Part Two': https://learn.microsoft.com/en-us/shows/history/history-of-microsoft-jeff-raikes-story-part-two

Steve Jobs and Bill Gates (1997). 'Steve Jobs and Bill Gates Together at D5 Conference 2007'. BrioWebTV (29 March 2013): https://www.youtube.com/watch?v=wvhW8cp15tk

Chapter 4

Bill Gates (1994). 'Keynote Speech "Information at your Fingertips" from Bill Gates at Comdex (1994) – Full Version'. Christoph Dernbach (15 November 2020): https://www.youtube.com/watch?v=-BQRFcQue_U

Steve Ballmer (4 November 2016). 'Microsoft's Former CEO Says Disagreement With Gates on Smartphones Drove Them Apart'. Bloomberg Technology: https://www.youtube.com/watch?v=qFe0S3F389w&t=285s

Chapter 5

World Economic Forum (25 January 2008). 'Davos Annual Meeting 2008 – Bill Gates': https://www.youtube.com/watch?v=Ql-Mtlx31e8

Stanford (16 June 2014). 'Bill and Melinda Gates' 2014 Stanford Commencement Address': https://www.youtube.com/watch?v=wug9n5Atk8c

CBS Mornings (3 March 2022). 'Melinda French Gates on having no regrets: "I gave every single piece of myself to this marriage"': https://www.youtube.com/watch?v=CTy7P9iEMbg

Today (3 May 2022). 'Exclusive: Bill Gates Talks Divorce, Jeffrey Epstein, Elon Musk': https://www.youtube.com/watch?v=X_qsgcjJ3-Y

BBC Radio 4 (3 February 2023). 'Amol Rajan Interviews … Bill Gates': https://www.bbc.co.uk/programmes/p0f0n47x

Chapter 6

CNBC Make It (February 26, 2019). 'Bill Gates Wasn't Worried About Burnout In 1984 – Here's Why': https://www.youtube.com/watch?v=MhnSzwXvGfc

Netflix (2018). *Inside Bill's Brain: Decoding Bill Gates*: https://www.netflix.com/gb/title/80184771

Quartz (10 October 2017). 'How Bill Gates reads books': https://www.youtube.com/watch?v=eTFy8RnUkoU

Harvard University (20 May 2013). 'Bill Gates Harvard Commencement Address 2007': https://www.youtube.com/watch?v=zPx5N6Lh3sw

Bloomberg Originals (24 February 2016). 'The One Thing Bill Gates Says Is Crucial for Success': https://www.youtube.com/watch?v=Dkexb3uJVgM

Fora.tv (6 May 2011). 'Bill Gates on Expertise: 10,000 Hours and a Lifetime of Fanaticism': https://www.youtube.com/watch?v=CsGihiSE6sM

Conclusion

World Economic Forum (25 January 2008). 'Davos Annual Meeting 2008 – Bill Gates': https://www.youtube.com/watch?v=Ql-Mtlx31e8

ABC News (8 May 2023). 'Bill Gates speaks out on artificial intelligence': https://abcnews.go.com/WNT/video/bill-gates-speaks-artificial-intelligence-99181293

BBC Radio 4 (3 February 2023). 'Amol Rajan Interviews … Bill Gates': https://www.bbc.co.uk/programmes/p0f0n47x

INDEX

Allen, Paul
  founds Microsoft 8
  in Lakeside
  Programmers Group
  27, 29, 30, 31–3, 34
  development of Altair
  BASIC 35–7, 38–9
  creation of Microsoft
  41–2
  break with MITS 46,
  47, 49, 50
  and SoftCard 62
  and MS-DOS 64, 66
  changing role in
  Microsoft 66
  relationship with Bill
  Gates 67–70
  leaves Microsoft 69
Allyn, Bobby 165
Altair BASIC 35–7, 38–9,
  42–50
Andreesen, Marc 105–6
Android (operating
  system) 130, 132
Aniston, Jennifer 110
Apple II 45, 51, 62
*Apple Computer,
  Inc. v. Microsoft
  Corporation* 93–4
Apple computers
  and Apple II 45, 51,
  62
  relationship with
  Microsoft 51, 80–2,
  90–9

goes public 73
Microsoft software
  applications for 77, 79
and graphical user
  interface 80
revival under Steve
  Jobs 124–5
and iPhone 130
Apple Macintosh, The
  (Lu) 53
Arnault, Berbard 12
Arnett, Nick 95
Arnold, Bridgitt 166
ASCII Corporation 58
Auletta, Ken 127
Austin, Dennis 78
Azure 10
Ballmer, Steve 57, 64, 67,
  69, 84, 89, 119, 120,
  121, 126, 130, 132,
  133–4
*Barbarians Led By Bill
  Gates: Microsoft from
  the Inside* (Edstrom &
  Eller) 85
BASIC (programming
  language) 11, 25, 26
  and Altair BASIC
  35–7, 38–9, 42–50
  and MS BASIC 50–1
Bennett, Jill 160
Berners-Lee, Tim 105
Bezos, Jeff 12, 72
Bill & Melinda Gates
  Foundation (BMGF)

12–13, 140–1, 146–56
Bina, Eric 105–6
Breakthrough Energy 158
Bricklin, Dan 61
Brock, Rod 65
Brodie, Richard 75
Buffett, Warren 138, 140
Bush, George H. W.
  103–4
*Business @ the Speed
  of Thought: Using
  a Digital Nervous
  System* (Gates) 171–8,
  186, 191
BusinessWeek 116
CBS Mornings 165–6
ChatGPT 10
Chu, Albert 56
Clark, Jim 106
COBOL (programming
  language) 24, 50
'Colossus' computer 22
Commodore PET 45
Computer Center
  Corporation (CEC)
  27–30
CP/M (operating system)
  62–3, 74
Davidoff, Monte 38, 39
Desert Island Discs (radio
  programme) 187
Digital Research 63, 64
Dudley, Brier 57
Duncan, Ray 54
Dynamical Systems

Research (DSR) 88
Edstrom, Jennifer 84–5
Electronic Numerical
    Integrator and
    Computer (ENIAC)
    22–3
Eller, Marlin 84–5
Epstein, Jeffrey 166
Erickson, Jim 18, 21, 32,
    35, 45, 48, 54, 63, 65,
    84, 94, 174, 175
Evans, Kent 27, 30, 32,
    33
Exploring the IBM PC
    (Norton) 53
Ferranti Mark 1 23
Flitter, Emily 166
Forbes (magazine) 119
FORTRAN
    (programming
    language) 24, 50
Fortune (magazine) 103
Gaskins, Robert 78
Gates, Bill
    founds Microsoft 8,
    41–2
    as 'inventor' 10–12
    and Bill & Melinda
    Gates Foundation
    12–13, 139, 140–1,
    146–9, 150–2, 155
    parental influence on
    17–19
    relationships with
    parents 20–1
    at Lakeside 21–2,
    30–1
    programming at

Lakeside 26–30, 31–4
    death of Kent Evan 33
    at Harvard University
    34–5, 48
    development of Altair
    BASIC 35–7, 38–9
    letter on software
    copyright 42–4
    break with MITS
    45–50
    activities in late 1970s
    51–3
    move to Seattle 55
    and Miriam Lubow
    56–7
    work ethic 59, 186–8
    arrest for speeding 59
    and move into
    software applications
    61–2, 73–4
    and MS-DOS 62, 63,
    64, 65
    changing role in
    Microsoft 66–7
    relationship with Paul
    Allen 67–70
    personal wealth of
    71–2
    and Microsoft Word
    76
and Microsoft Excel 77
and Microsoft
    PowerPoint 79
and Apple computers
    80–2, 90–1, 92, 94–9
and Microsoft Windows
    82–6
and IBM 87–8, 89

influence of 103–4
    and rise of the internet
    104, 106, 107–9
    and Windows 95 110
    antitrust case against
    Microsoft 112–14,
    116–17
relationship with Melinda
    Gates 118–19, 158–9,
    162–7
    steps down as
    Microsoft CEO
    119–21, 134
    at launch of Windows
    Vista 122–3
    and XBox 126–7, 128
    failure in smartphone
    market 130, 132–3
    marks fortieth
    anniversary of
    Microsoft 134–6
    at World Economic
    Forum 137–8
    takes Giving Pledge
    138–40
    and Gates Library
    Foundation 143–4
    work in developing
    world 144–6, 154
    position on equality
    issues 147–9
    and climate change
    155–8
    girlfriends of 160–3
    approach to business
    170–9
    personal recipe for
    success 179–89

optimistic view of
191–5
view of artificial
intelligence 193–4
Gates, Jennifer (BG's
daughter) 119
Gates, Kristi (BG's sister)
20
Gates, Libby (BG's sister)
20
Gates, Mary (BG's
mother) 16–17, 19,
20–1, 48, 62, 164
Gates, Melinda (BG's
wife) 118–19, 138,
140, 141, 144, 146,
147, 154, 158–9,
162–7
Gates, Phoebe (BG's
daughter) 119
Gates, Rory (BG's son)
119
Gates, William Snr. (BG's
father) 16, 18–19,
20–1
Gates Learning
Foundation 144
Gates Library
Foundation 143–4
Gavi: The Vaccine
Alliance 146, 149–50
General Electric 47
Gibbons, Frank 81
Giving Pledge 138–40
Gladwell, Malcolm 188
Global Polio Eradication
Initiative (GPEI) 150
Gloyd, Karen 35

Google 128–9
Guth, Robert 183
Hanson, Rowland 75, 82
*Hard Drive: Bill Gates
and the Making
of the Microsoft
Empire* (Wallace and
Erickson) 18, 21, 54
Harvard University 34–5,
48
*Homebrew Computer
Club Newsletter* 42
Hopper, Grace 24
*How to Avoid Climate
Disaster: The
Solutions We Have
and the Breakthroughs
We Need* (Gates) 157
*How to Prevent the Next
Pandemic* (Gates) 152
Huddleston, Tom 82
IBM 23–4, 24–5, 59–60,
62–6, 83, 86–8,
89–90
IBM 701 Electronic Data
Processing Machine
23–4
Idea Man: A Memoir
by the Co-founder
of Microsoft (Allen)
68, 69
Idei, Nobuyuki 127
Information Sciences Inc.
31–2
*InfoWorld: The PC News
Weekly* 95
*Inside Bill's Brain:
Decoding Bill Gates*

(documentary) 33, 194
Integer BASIC 51
International Computers
Limited 58
Internet Explorer 106–7,
111–12
iPhone 130
Isaacson, Walter 11, 90
Jarvis, Rebecca 193
JAVA 115
Jazz (spreadsheet) 77
Jobs, Steve 11, 51, 81, 90,
97–8, 124
Johnston, Stuart 96
Jones, Rashida 148–9
Kapor, Mitch 81
Kastrenakes, Jacob 134
Kelly, Kevin 172
Kemeny, John G. 11, 25
Kilby, Jack 24
Kildall, Gary 61, 62–3
King, Gayle 165–6
Koninklijke Philips N.V.
58
Kurtz, Thomas E. 11, 25
Lakeside (prep school)
21–2, 25–30, 31–4
Lakeside Mothers' Club
26
Lakeside Programmers
Group (LPG) 27–9,
31–2, 33
Lammers, Susan 52–3
Larson, Chris 39
Logic Simulation
Company (LSC) 33
Lotus 1-2-3 74–5, 77
Lu, Cary 53

Lubow, Miriam 55, 56–7
MacDonald, Marc 54
MacGregor, Scott 82
Maher, Jimmy 64
McEwen, Dorothy 63
Myhrvold, Nathan 108–9
Micro Instrumentation
    and Telemetry (MITS)
    37, 38–9, 41, 44–50
MicroPro International
    61
Microsoft
    dominance of 8–10,
    103
    and MS-DOS 11, 54,
    62–6, 74
creation of 41–2
    break from MITS
    44–50
    and MS BASIC 50–1
    relationship with
    Apple computers 51,
    80–2, 90–9
    move to Seattle 55–6
    in international
    markets 58
    and IBM 59–60,
    62–6, 86–8, 89–90
    and Seattle Computer
    Products 60–1
    starts developing
    software applications
    61–2, 73–4
    restructure in 1981
    66–7
    goes public 71
    and Microsoft Word
    75–7

and Microsoft Excel
    77
and rise of the internet
    104, 106–7
and Internet Explorer
    106–7, 111–12
antitrust case against
    112–18
BG steps down as
    CEO 119–21, 134
and XBox 126–8
failure in smartphone
    market 129–30, 132–3
fortieth anniversary of
    134–6
Microsoft Excel 77
Microsoft PowerPoint
    78–9
Microsoft Press 52, 53–4
Microsoft Windows
    dominance of 10
    launch of 9, 85–6
    Windows 3.0 76–7,
    79, 89, 96
    development of 82–5,
    88–90, 121–2
    and IBM 87–8
    Windows 95 109–12
    Windows Vista 121–4
Microsoft Word 75–7
Mission Innovation 158
Mohr, Ian 140
Mosaic (browser) 106,
    107
MS-DOS 11, 54, 62–6,
    74
MS-DOS Technical
    Reference

Encyclopedia 54
MS Office 79
Multiplan 74
Musk, Elon 12
Nadella, Satya 134
National Cash Register
    (NCR) 47
Netscape Navigator 106,
    111–12, 114
Neuborne, Ellen 116
Nintendo 125
Nishi, Kazuhiko 'Kay' 58
Noe, Bernie 181
Norton, Peter 53
Noyce, Robert 24
Opel, John R. 62
Open Handset Alliance
    (OHA) 130
'Open Letter to
    Hobbyists' 42–4
O'Rear, Bob 61, 64
OS/2 86–8, 89–90
Outliers: The Story of
    Success (Gladwell) 188
Palmer, Scott 95
Paterson, Tim 61, 64, 65
Pauley, Jane 48, 179
Perry, Matthew 110
Pertec Computer
    Corporation (PCC)
    49–50
PlayStation 125, 127
Politico (website) 150
Popular Electronics 36,
    41
Programmers at Work
    (Lammers) 52–3
Quarterdeck 83

R2E 58
Raburn, Vern 61
Raikes, Jeff 78
Rajan, Amol 167, 194–5
Reinvent the Toilet
    challenge 153
Rinearson, Peter 109
Road Ahead, The (Gates
    et al.) 108–9
Roberts, Ed 37, 39, 174
Roberston, Alexander
    187
Rusche, Dominic 69
Salo, Jackie 161
Sams, Jack 62, 63
San Francisco Chronicle
    161
San Jose Mercury News
    94–5
Sargent, Murray 88
Satellite Software
    International (SSI) 61
Scoglio, Chris 127
Scott, Ridley 80
Sculley, John 78, 91, 94
Seattle Computer
    Products (SCP) 60–1,
    64–5
Sheehy, Kate 161
*Silicon Valley Business
    Journal* 162
Simonyi, Charles 65, 75,
    76, 82
Slade, Mike 181
Smith, Steve 61–2
SoftCard 62
Sony 126–7
Sound Families 146

Spyglass Inc. 107, 111
Standalone Disk BASIC
    62
*Steve Jobs: The Exclusive
    Biography* (Isaacson)
    90
Stewart, James 166
Stroum, Samuel N. 48
Suzman, Mark 151
Tandy TRS-80 45
Thunberg, Greta 194
Time (magazine) 97, 114
Today (radio programme)
    167
TopView 83
Towne, James 67
'Traf-O-Data' project
    32–3
TRS-80 50–1
TRW 33–4
Tsukamoto, Keiichiro 58
Vector International 58
VisiCalc 61, 74
VisiCorp 83
Wall Street Journal 69,
    183
Wallace, James 18, 21,
    32, 35, 45, 48, 54, 63,
    65, 84, 94, 107, 114,
    159, 163, 164, 174,
    175
Washington Post 15
Weiland, Richard 27,
    31–2
Weiss, Dave 88, 89
Winbald, Ann 161–3
Windows 95 109–12
Windows Mobile 129–30

Windows Vista 121–4
Wood, Marla 57
Wood, Steve 56–7
WordPerfect 61, 76, 77
WordStar 61, 76, 77
World Economic Forum
    (WEF) 137–8, 192
Wozniak, Steve 51
XBox 9, 126–8
Xerox 11, 62, 80, 96
Xerox Alto 80
Xerox PARC 79–80
Yudkowsky, Eliezer 193